Steve Colgate
on
Cruising

The hows and whys of bareboat chartering or cruising on your own.

WRITTEN BY: STEVE COLGATE
CEO., OFFSHORE SAILING SCHOOL, LTD.

ILLUSTRATIONS BY: MIKE DICKEY

D0041434

Reprinted 1995, 2005

Published in 1990 by Steve Colgate
Offshore Sailing School, Ltd.
16731 McGregor Blvd.
Ft. Myers, FL   33908
800–221–4326

ISBN 0–914747–01–0

CONTENTS

Thanks to Tyler Pierce for his
practical contributions to this book.

Chapter 1

BAREBOAT CHARTERING

In 1972, shortly after the concept evolved of making a fleet of cruising sailboats available for individual sailors to charter without captains (bareboat), Offshore Sailing School, Ltd. chartered four identical boats and took a group of graduates to The Moorings in the British Virgin Islands for a week of cruising. Thus the concept of "flotilla cruising" was born. Before this time such an idea was virtually impossible because one couldn't find enough similar boats in one location to charter for a group.

Since 1972, Offshore has led close to 70 cruises including such cruising grounds as Greece, Turkey, France, Tahiti, Maine, Rhode Island, Chesapeake, San Juan Islands, Apostle Islands, Belize, Honduras, Sea of Cortez, Florida Keys, Guadaloupe, Grenadines, St. Martin, many of them multiple years at one location. We've seen some charter agencies improve and expand while others have withered and died. We've learned what to expect from cruising exotic spots and what causes the most problems. Our purpose in this book is to give you the knowledge you will need to comfortably charter bareboat (without a captain) from one of the charter fleets. The boat you charter may be worth close to $400,000. Obviously a charter company will be very careful about who is capable of taking on such a responsibility.

CHOOSING A CHARTER COMPANY

Over the years of chartering from various bareboat charter fleets we've encountered the good, the bad and the indifferent. Some of the early leaders have gone downhill because of too much expansion, too little capitalization or too much competition. The bareboat charter field is flooded with companies. Generally the largest are the most reliable and I wouldn't be surprised if the whole charter market coalesces into three or four major players. The Moorings, one of the largest charter companies, has seven branches in the Caribbean, one each in the Bahamas, Sea of Cortez, Belize, Tahiti, Tonga, Australia, Seychelles and 12 branches in the Mediterranean.

Our experiences have been best where a charter company has complete control and responsibility for the boats they charter. In some cases, privately owned personal boats are managed for a fee or a commission by a charter company. This is fine for the charter company which doesn't have to make large capital investments or pay lease payments whether or not the income covers it, but often poor for the charterer because the charter company has little control over the standards. Each boat is different, so backup spares are difficult to stock. When a company has a relationship with a sailboat dealer, the privately owned boats are predominantly of the makes the dealer sells which is a step towards standardization.

Many people have been burned by choosing a charter company based on price alone. The charter business is a highly competitive business, so an outfit that's slashing price must, by the nature of the business, slash service and maintenance. Perhaps you are willing to deal with a boat full of roaches for a low price and if that's all that happens, fine. The risk is the company may go out of business as many have, before you get your charter and in that case you have lost your 50% deposit that you may have put down six months out to reserve the boat or the full payment that is due before the cruise. You may also lose the money paid for non-refundable airline tickets. Some charter companies have insurance policies you can buy that protects you from loss of money paid to them in case of a sickness or death in your family. They don't protect you for the charter company's bankruptcy, so that risk is still there.

Another risk with marginal companies is the money you put up front as a refundable security deposit. This usually is a sum equal to the insurance deductible on the boat, so if there's any loss during your cruise, they can take it out of the security deposit and return the balance to you or if the boat is a total loss, they have the deductible amount from you and won't be out of pocket to the insurance company. The security deposit can be $500 to $900 on a charter cruise that costs you $1500 to $2000 for a week. With all the operating costs a charter company has, that security money is often being used for overhead expenses. After all, it's 30% or more of all income. Then with marginal companies, new security deposits are used to pay back old ones, meaning that you may have to wait quite a while to get it back. In the case of one cruise it took us three months after the cruise to get our security deposits returned and only with many letters, calls and finally resorting to threats that we would cast aspersions on their reputation in the industry. In another recent example, a company we had used successfully a couple of times previously held on to our security deposits, charged us a cleanup charge for boats we received dirty in the first place and tried to trump up a number of other charges. We finally got most of our security deposit back after two months, but there's no real recourse if you disagree with the amounts taken out. Besides, if the company goes bankrupt, the security deposit is lost too.

An American company called the Charter Yacht Brokers Association (CYBA) can help if you deal through a yacht broker rather than with the charter company directly. The association holds escrow deposits for the brokers rather than sending them to the charterer. Some bareboat companies don't deal through brokers who take a 10% commission, so the CYBA can't help in those cases.

The best advice is to look into the charter company you are planning to charter from very carefully. Ask for some names of references of people who have chartered from them in the near past if you have any doubts. Use companies that friends have used and have had good experiences with. Talk to people in the industry. Call a sailing magazine for advice.

CRUISE PREPARATION

Once you have chosen the area you want to cruise, you need to select the time of year. Most areas of the world have periods of unsettled weather certain months of the year. You may ask the charter company which months to avoid and they should be honest with you, but remember they want to charter as much as possible, including rainy times, so they may paint a rosier picture than they should. A very good source is the sailing guide book for the area. For the Caribbean and Baja California a good source is "Cruising Guide Publications," PO Box 1017, Dunedin, FL 34697-1017. If you charter with The Moorings, they will send you the appropriate guide. Don Street is an indefatigable writer of good cruising guides for the Caribbean. For "Down East" we use

Roger Duncan and John Ware's "A Cruising Guide to the New England Coast" by Dodd, Mead & Co. H.M. Denbam has written more excellent guides of Greece and the Aegean. An English company named Laurie Norie & Wilson, LTD of Wych House St. Ives, Cambridgeshire, England has created the best guides I have ever seen of the Mediterranean including Spain, Portugal, France, Italy, Turkey, Greece and Yugoslavia. You can usually obtain these and similar guide books through stores that sell nautical charts.

The information found in these guides includes average rainfall, the local winds, their force and direction and the average number of days a month sailors might experience a "bora", a "mistral", a "sirocco", a "meltemi" or other winds with mystical names you'd rather read about than encounter.

Another good source of wind information are pilot charts. They are printed for each month of the year for various areas of the world. Locate your cruising area for the intended month of your cruise and look at the wind rose there. Figure 1 is the pilot chart for the Mediterranean Sea in July. Look at the wind rose for the southwest coast of Turkey, one of Offshore Cruising Club's overseas cruises. The arrows fly with the wind, the tails indicating the direction from which the wind is blowing. The length of the arrow shaft measured from the outside of the circle to the end of the visible shaft, using the scale in figure 1, gives the percentage of the total number of observations that the wind blows from that direction. The number of feathers show the average force of the wind on the Beaufort Scale (figure 2). The number in the center of the circle gives the percentage of calms for the month. Look at the wind rose in figure 1. For Turkey in July we can expect 3% calms. The winds will be 3% from the east, 4% from the SE, 4% from the south, 4% form the SW. All these wind direction arrows have three feathers, indicating force 3 (7 to 10 knots). 23% of the winds will come from the west, 30% from the NW, 21% from the north, and 8% from the NE. All these winds will average force 4 (11 to 16 knots).

The Pilot Chart also gives information about the frequency of storms and fog, the height of waves, the local air and water temperature, and the ocean current among other things.

The Beaufort Scale is used more widely in Europe than in the U.S., so I have devised a quick conversion formula to wind speed in knots to make it easier for us to understand European weather reports.

Note that there are thirteen forces (0–12) in the Beaufort Wind Scale. Just remember "3-4-5". To convert them to knots, multi-

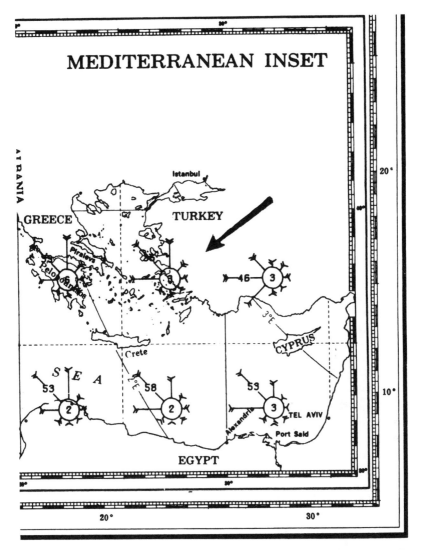

JULY 1988 16
DMA STOCK NO.
PILOT168807.

Figure 1

FIGURE 2

BEAUFORT WIND SCALE

BEAUFORT FORCE	WINDSPEED KNOTS
0	UNDER 1
1	1–3
2	4–6
3	7–10
4	11–16
5	17–21
6	22–27
7	28–33
8	34–40
9	41–47
10	48–55
11	56–63
12	64 AND OVER

ply the first four force levels (0–3) by 3, the second four (4–7) by 4, and the next four (8–11) by 5. The result is a figure in knots that falls within the range of knots for that force level. For instance, force 6 times 4 is 24 knots. The range for force 6 is 22–27 knots. Then just remember that force 12 is 64 knots and over.

ITINERARY

After you have read about the area, it's a good idea to develop a tentative itinerary. Unfortunately, you don't have unlimited time, so if you are returning the sailboat to the same location you started from, you can't afford to get too far away, particularly downwind. Given a certain prevailing wind direction, I suggest the first day or two be easy reaches, so everybody can unwind, get their sea legs and recover from jet lag, if any. Next work your way upwind in fairly short hops. Save the long stretches for reaches and runs. Then having reached the furthest point from the base, start back downwind. Usually check-in time at the end of the cruise is about noon, so plan on spending the last night within about five miles of the charter base. This allows you time to clean the boat before returning it. I was always brought up that you return a boat in as good or better condition than you received it and we try to impart that concept to all our students and cruise participants. There's a monetary motivation also. Most charter companies will charge an extra cleaning fee if a boat is left in an abnormally dirty condition. Don't consider your boat as a hotel room that you can trash and leave. Be proud in the seamanship of returning it spotless.

DISTANCES

Don't try to sail too far. Figure roughly a five knot average speed and that 3 to 6 hours of sailing a day will satisfy most tastes. This keeps the distances in the 15 to 30 mile range between ports. Remember that the joy of cruising is sightseeing by water. Instead of having to pack and unpack every night at a different hotel and board a bus, train or plane every day, you are taking your hotel room with you. Allow enough time to enjoy the history, the food and the customs of each port you visit. If you only want to go out and pound twelve hours to windward, save it for a race at home.

NUMBER OF BERTHS

The number of people you go with on the cruise should not be dependent simply on the number of berths available on the boat. In Europe, people are used to being crowded. There isn't the sense of space we Americans are used to. European condos, apartments, houses and hotel rooms all tend to be smaller than in the U.S. So the Europeans will advertise 8 berths in a 35' sailboat, 10 berths in a 43 footer or 12 berths in a 50 footer. If these same boats were chartered by Offshore for a cruise, we would assign 4, 6, and 8 sailors respectively to the 35', 43', 50' sailboat. Generally, even when sailing alone with friends, six is a nice number. It keeps the cost of the cruise more reasonable and if one couple wants to be alone or doesn't want to participate in sightseeing or sailing two couples still have each other for camaraderie.

SECURITY DEPOSIT

We've mentioned the fact that many charter companies require a security deposit equal to the insurance deductible on the boat you are chartering. They then take out of the deposit any items that are lost or missing after the cruise. Because people are becoming wary of putting up such a large hunk of money and because of the problems that have occasionally occurred in getting the money back, some more progressive charter companies have come up with a new system. A well run charter company with good equipment usually has minimal losses, so they, in essence, "self-insure" for losses up to the insurance deductible by giving the charterer the option of a non-refundable insurance premium of approximately $10 a day or a refundable security deposit of a lump sum such as $900. When you get aboard your chartered sailboat, you will be given a list of items of equipment you are responsible for. Check it carefully and make sure everything they list is aboard. Beyond the list, check if there is any pre-existing damage to the boat such as bent stanchions or scratches and chips in the topsides gelcoat. I like to check the bottom of the keel at the first swimming opportunity so if the boat has obviously been grounded, I will have a rebuttal to any accusations that we might have been responsible. I have never found such a defense necessary, because the charter company usually knows which of their boats have gone aground and when.

PACKING FOR THE CRUISE

The majority of bareboat charter companies are located in warm vacation spots, so the need to carry a lot of warm clothing is rare. Stack on a bed the clothes you might go through at best in warm weather. Then cut the stack in half and you still are probably taking too much. In other words, travel light. Pack in soft duffels, because there's no storage place on a boat for hard luggage. Plus, any charter company staff that sees a person going aboard with hard luggage will instantly question that person's experience and sailing ability. Mark your name and address on the duffels with an indelible broad tip marker. It's better to carry two small duffels rather than packing all your clothes in one large one. You tend to "live out of your duffels" on a short cruise and it's a mess to get to the bottom of one large duffel.

We highly recommend taking a carry-on duffel with you on the plane rather than checking all your luggage. Then, if your baggage is lost, you at least have a couple of shorts, shirts, swim suit, underwear, and toilet kit. Once you start the cruise you can't go back to check the airport daily. That's one of the nice things about the group cruising we do. There's always a few people that might be willing to lend more clothing to the poor soul who's luggage was lost.

If you need to wear eyeglasses, an extra pair could come in handy. For sailing, eyeglass straps are a must so bring them for each pair. Be sure to bring any prescription drugs you need, because they may be hard to find in the cruising area if you forget them. We usually carry Lomotil for diarrhea. You never can tell when "the revenge" might hit. Ever since I picked up a cold during the Bermuda Race and flew from Bermuda to New York with it I've been carrying Afrin nosedrops in my kit. The pressure change when descending into New York was excruciating, because I couldn't clear my ears. I couldn't clear the blockage even on the ground and it quickly became infected. Antibiotics cleared it up, but the doctor suggested Afrin when flying with a cold. I have since flown with colds and a couple of squirts in the nose with Afrin just before going up and just before coming down have prevented a reccurrence of the problem.

If you are taking a medication, check with your doctor that it isn't sun sensitive. I was taking Tetracycline one time for a skin condition and went on a cruise of the Virgin Islands. About the third day out I began feeling very nauseous, just like seasickness. Since I had never before been seasick in such mild conditions, I guessed it must be the Tetracycline. I stopped taking it and the symptoms disappeared quickly.

A good sun lotion is important, so bring one along. Use an SPF (Sun Protection Factor) of at least 15, particularly if you're fair skinned or haven't been exposed to sun much recently. Test before hand that you aren't allergic to PABA now used in many lotions.

Bring sailing gloves to avoid rope burn and blisters. Once you have them, they will take a long time to heal with the salt water exposure.

Don't run out of film. If you have to buy color film in a foreign country, it can be very expensive. Also, the type you want may not be readily available. Bring more that you think you may use and you'll probably wind up about right. As for airport X-ray machines, we have been through lots of them with 20–30 rolls of both color and black and white film, exposed and unexposed, without any discernible diminishing of quality of the finished photographs. However, we don't use film with an ASA higher than 200. I gather if you use fast film, 400 ASA or higher, you should start being concerned about its exposure to airport X-ray machines. The following is a checklist that may be helpful for packing. Quantities have been left out because that depends on the length of the cruise.

CHECKLIST WARM
WEATHER CRUISE*

Shorts   Camera, film, lens cleaners
Swim suits   (1) Hand bearing compass
Long pants   (1) Binoculars
Underwear   Sunglasses
Knit shirts   Regular eye glasses
Belt   Eyeglass straps
Light jacket (windbreaker)   Paperbacks
Sailing gloves   (2) Snorkel & mask
Visor, hat, lanyard   Passport, visa if necessary
Toilet kit, medicines   Air tickets
Boat shoes   (3) Music CD's
Socks   Cash
                                ATM Card and PIN
                                Sunscreen or sunblock
                                Beer can insulators

*Colder weather add: foulweather gear, wool socks, boots, heavy jacket, sweater, sweatshirts.

(1) Most charterboats have hand bearing compasses and binoculars but they usually aren't very good. Bring them if you have a favorite.
(2) Fins and masks are almost always provided by the charter agency, but definitely check before going. Masks sometimes don't fit a small or narrow face well. Bring your own if you have a favorite that fits well
(3) Most charter boats have CD players, so bring the music you enjoy.

CUSTOMS AND PASSPORTS

Some people forget when they visit a small country that the customs and immigration officials can make life very difficult if they have a mind to. After all, it is their country you're visiting and if you are a wise guy, they might just send you home on the next plane. Being polite and respectful is important even if you feel you are being provoked. When you return to the U.S. declare all you've bought with the U.S. Customs. I know people who have been caught not declaring and were put in the computer. For years, every time they came back into the U.S. they were thoroughly searched. It's not worth the risk of years of continual humiliation and aggravation just to save the 10% duty after you've used up your free allowance. You might think that art and antiques are free of duty, but there are many classes and categories. Though you may know an antique is over 100 years old and not dutiable, you may be asked to prove it with written documentation of an accredited appraiser.

CURRENCY

We used to change U.S. dollars for foreign exchange in the U.S. before leaving, at the arrival airport, at destination hotels and at currency exchange shops. Few of these gave a decent exchange rate. Now the world has changed and ATM's are "king". Recently we traveled to Europe and took with us a number $100 bills. No bank would change them unless you had an account and the rate we received at the airport was terrible. We relied on ATM's for cash and they were everywhere. In the little town of Finikas on Syros, Greece we lead a flotilla cruise of five boats of our grads. In the week that we were gone, a new ATM was planted at the one street corner. Make sure before you leave the U.S. that you have a workable PIN number for your card.

DRUGS

If you dabble with drugs at home, don't even think of taking them on any cruise. Our instructors are directed to kick off the boat any person taking drugs. The reason is simple. All bareboat charter contracts have clauses to the effect that if the boat is used for illegal purposes, the charterer is totally responsible for whatever happens to the boat. Insurance is voided, so the deductible is not applicable. If the authorities come on the boat and impound it under the U.S.'s "Zero Tolerance" policies, the charter company will go after the person that caused the impounding for the full price of the boat which could be over $400,000. Even if the authorities give the boat back, the person is responsible for: 1) legal fees 2) repair of the boat (the search for additional drugs may cause the interior to be demolished) 3) storage fees when impounded and 4) loss of charter revenues to the charter company. All this could result from the smoking of one joint of marijuana or even having the residue of some marijuana in your toilet kit, for instance. And don't think it's any better in other countries. You've all heard what Turkish jails are like for the possessors of drugs, and the Indonesian death penalty. Even in the beautiful, civilized British Virgin Islands, drugs are a quick way to a long jail term.

CHECKOUTS

Every charter company in the world will have a checkout, but they vary in emphasis. In Europe, the emphasis is on the actual operation of the equipment on the boat. In the Caribbean, the emphasis has changed over the years to be very heavy on navigation and anchoring. By navigation we mean which areas on the chart to avoid and the best approach into harbors. They believe that if you can find a harbor each day and stay there all night after you've found it, your cruise will be a success. The Europeans assume that you have all that basic knowledge and are more concerned that you don't mess up the boat because of unfamiliarity with its operation.

The licensing factor is becoming a big problem for Americans bareboat chartering in Europe after unification. A cruising license is mandatory for the skipper and the stringent requirements will be uniform throughout Europe. At present the charter companies in Europe issue a license in those countries that require one, so don't be concerned.

PROVISIONING AND STOWING GEAR

After a chart checkout and a boat checkout, you will need to stow your gear and provisions. In the Caribbean, you are now apt to cook aboard. In the Med., we dined ashore almost every night. The charter company will usually provision for you if you request their service, but will not stow the food. You need to stow it yourselves, so you'll know what you have and where it can be found. Fresh eggs don't have to be refrigerated, though they shouldn't be kept in a warm place. We raced from Marblehead, Massachusetts to Cork, Ireland one year and had perfectly good eggs after the finish, 15 days old, which we had kept in a locker. But fresh baked bread usually doesn't have preservatives in countries where we cruise and needs to be kept in the refrigerator. Mayonnaise, even opened, can be kept in a locker. Fruit can be in plastic bags in the refrigerator, but not outside in the cabin. The plastic bags accelerate rotting. Wrap heads of wet lettuce in aluminum foil and keep them in the refrigerator. The foil will keep the lettuce from spoiling for weeks. Don't let lettuce, fruit or tomatoes come in direct contact with the cold plates or ice because they will "burn" where they touch.

As mentioned earlier, you will be given a checklist of items the charter company has put on the boat. Besides making sure you have everything, by checking off the items you learn where they are when needed as in an emergency. Always have every crew member learn where the fire extinguishers are so they can be found in a hurry. Figure 3 is a photo Doris and I took of a 33 foot fiberglass chartered sailboat in the British Virgin Islands. The

FIGURE 3

FIRE ON A CHARTER SAILBOAT IN THE BRITISH VIRGIN ISLANDS OFF TORTOLA. A SICKENING SIGHT.

boat burned down to the waterline. Fire is the most frightening thing one can think of on a sailboat (except possibly an explosion). Once the flashpoint of fiberglass is reached, it burns as easily as wood. Fire can come from unexpected sources. We had a diesel engine fire on a chartered boat once because the starter motor's bendix drive didn't disengage after the engine started. We put it out immediately by stopping the engine and spraying it with a dry chemical fire extinguisher, but not before some very anxious moments.

Other things you should note on your checklist are the location of the various thru-hull fittings, so you can quickly close the valve if a hose clamp or a hose breaks. Note the location of life vests, flares, the emergency tiller and the first aid kit.

Chapter 2

ON THE CRUISE:

BATTERY AND ELECTRICAL

Since every charter company has slightly different engine and battery procedures listen carefully during this part of the checkout. Sailboats used to have a master switch that selected banks of batteries. You charged and used one bank of batteries one day for your engine and lighting and the other the next. At last electrical systems have come of age with circuit breaker panels and separate batteries for lighting (the "house" battery) and engine starting. When the engine is running all batteries are being charged, but nothing draws the engine battery except starting. The breaker panel usually has a battery condition check, so you can determine if they are low.

ENGINE CHECKS

A diesel engine requires three components to run: fuel, air and compression. If there are troubles starting an engine, 90 percent of the time it's because of fuel. Fuel goes from the fuel tank to a primary filter with a water separator. Since water is heavier than diesel fuel, it sinks to the bottom of a cup and the water can be drained out. Large particles are also taken out by this filter. Next the fuel goes through a fuel lift pump which can be operated manually to push fuel through the system. Then it passes through a secondary filter which has a bleed point and on to the injector pump. The tolerances are very tight for the injector pump, so don't fool with it unless you are a qualified mechanic. This deliv-

ers diesel fuel at high pressure to the injectors which spray atom-
ized fuel into the cylinders where it mixes with air, is compressed
and ignites. If you have cleaned the fuel filters and have bled the
air bubbles out of the fuel system, but the engine still won't start,
lack of air could be the problem.

There is an air filter that may need to be cleaned so air can mix
with the fuel. The last problem could be lack of compression, but
there's not much that can be done about it without a total engine
rebuild. This usually comes from the engine being run without
oil or from overheating.

Check the oil level in the engine every morning. Look at it's
color. Oil should be jet black in a diesel. If it's milky grey, water is
in the oil. Also check the fresh water cooling level. Add if needed,
but be sure not to put water in the oil receptacle or oil in the
water reservoir. It's been done before, believe me. Some charter
companies will ask you to check the level of hydraulic fluids.
They will point out the proper dip stick and when to add fluid.
When you turn the key, loud engine alarms should sound which
stop as soon as the oil pressure gets up to the operative range. In
cooler climates you may have to hold a "preheat" button before
you press the starter button. After starting the engine, warm it up
for a few minutes before using it under load (in gear). Check the
oil pressure, water temperature and that water is coming out of
the exhaust. Circulating sea water cools the fresh water cooling
system and if there's no flow coming out of the exhaust, possibly
the raw water pump impeller is burned out or the intake thru
hull valve is closed or plugged with seaweed. The impeller is
made of rubber so the pump won't be damaged if sand is sucked
in. Next check the raw water strainer is clean of seaweed and the
cap is seated correctly. If the cap is not tight air can get into the
line and overheating results.

If the checkout is being presented by a person whose native
language isn't English, question anything that doesn't seem right.
We were told in Yugoslavia that after the engine was running we
could turn off the key. We questioned this statement but it was
confirmed. Either the checker was misled himself or he meant
you could turn off the key without hurting the engine or alterna-
tors. By turning off the key, however, we lost all our gauges and
alarms, so I quickly spread it around the rest of our flotilla to
disregard his statement and always leave the key on. Later in the
trip we lost our oil and wouldn't have known if the key had been
turned off.

ENGINE OPERATION

In the operation of the engine, shifting into or out of gear should always be done with the throttle at idle. With the single lever Morse control, this is automatic. The handle is pulled out at the center and when pushed forward, will rev up in neutral. When pulled back to the vertical position, it should pop in automatically. Then when you push it forward from neutral, it first goes into forward gear and then accelerates more and more the further you push the handle. Pull the handle back to put it into reverse and the farther you pull it back the more it accelerates in reverse. Problems arise when people jam it forward fast, then pull it back, reving it in reverse without pausing when the handle is vertical. It's terribly rough on the transmission. So treat it gently. Put it forward just enough to hear it "clunk" into forward gear before reving it up and when you pull back, pause with the handle in neutral, then pull back just enough to hear the engine "clunk" into reverse before pulling it back for speed.

Some handles have a button in the middle that you press and push the handle forward to rev in neutral. When you pull the handle back to vertical, the button pops out automatically, allowing the handle to engage in forward or reverse.

Modern sailboats are lighter than a few years ago and the engines are developing more horsepower with less weight and volume than before. This means modern sailboats will accelerate faster under power and stop faster when you put them in reverse. It's a good idea to practice under power the first day, so you know how long it takes to stop, how well the boat tracks in reverse, how it pulls when you gun it in reverse, what sort of turning radius you have and how much the wind will affect you when you make a circle under power. A good exercise is to try to make a perfect circle. Normally, the wind will cause the circle to be egg-shaped, but by advancing the throttle as you turn upwind and throttling back as you turn downwind, with practice you'll control the shape of the circle

Now practice making a tight full circle in forward gear to port and then to starboard. The boat will turn in a smaller radius to port than to starboard. This is because of the direction of rotation of the propeller. A propeller that rotates clockwise in forward gear is correctly called a right-hand wheel. Imagine it as a wheel that rests on the sea bottom. Clockwise rotation would "walk" the stern to starboard in forward gear and to port in reverse as in figure 4. For single engined sailboats, a right hand wheel is almost universally accepted. Should your boat have a left hand wheel, it will act opposite to the following examples.

I have talked to several architects, engine manufacturers, propeller engineers and read articles on why "prop walk" occurs and am not satisfied with any answer. Among the answers are: 1. Unequal blade thrust between ascending and descending blades because of the downward angle of the shaft 2. torque 3. disturbed water near the hull on the upper half of the blade rotation isn't as effective as the lower half and 4. more pressure at greater depths. Regardless of the true reason, think of the blades as having greater bite at the bottom of the rotation than at the top, so in forward the stern walks to starboard and in reverse it walks to port.

Next, practice making a tight, full circle in reverse gear to port and then to starboard. Note how much tighter the turn is to port than to starboard for the same reason as above.

By using the knowledge we now have of the difference in forward and reverse in both directions, we can use forward and reverse gear to make the smallest possible circle in each direction. This can be very handy knowledge if you are powering into a small harbor to look for an open slip, find nothing and need to do a 180 degree turn to exit the harbor.

Try a turn to starboard as in figure 5. Put the helm over to starboard to initiate the turn with the engine in neutral. Reverse

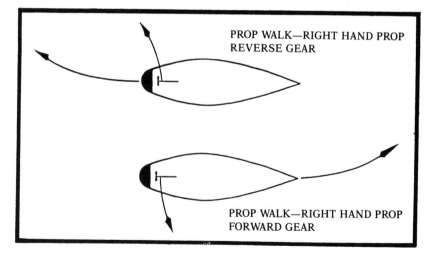

FIGURE 4

PROP WALK EFFECT IN FORWARD AND REVERSE GEAR

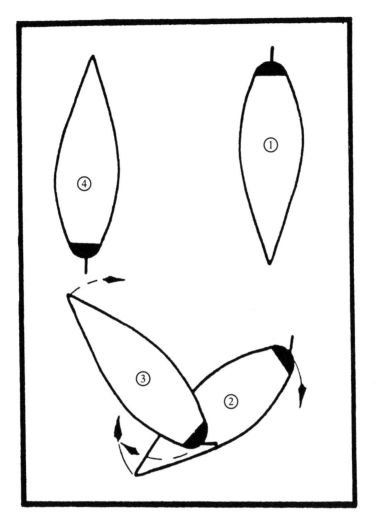

FIGURE 5

TURN TO STARBOARD

(1) APPROACHING THE TURN AREA, ENGINE IS IN NEUTRAL TO DECREASE SPEED.
(2) AS TURN IS INITIATED WITH RUDDER HARD TO STARBOARD, BURSTS OF REVERSE ARE APPLIED TO A) LOSE ALL FORWARD WAY AND B) PROP-WALK THE STERN TO PORT.
(3) WHEN BOAT HAS LOST ALL WAY, A BURST OF FORWARD WITH THE WHEEL STILL HARD OVER WILL COMPLETE THE TURN. IN THIS INSTANCE,THE NORMAL TENDENCY FOR THE BOW TO TURN TO PORT IN FORWARD IS OVERCOME BY PROPELLER WASH AGAINST THE RUDDER.
(4) THE TURN IS COMPLETED.

the engine with short bursts of power, leaving the helm hard over. You should be able to turn the boat completely around in little more than her boat length. If the boat starts going backwards you may need a few spurts in forward to complete the turn.

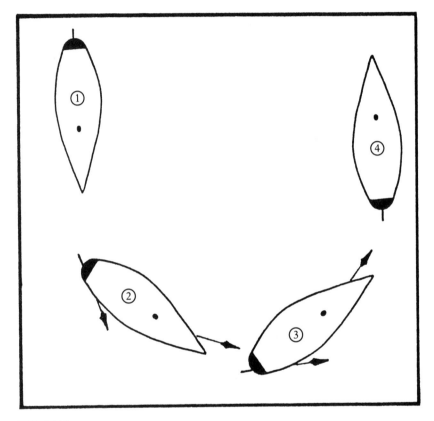

FIGURE 6

TURN TO PORT

(1) APPROACHING THE TURN, ENGINE IS IN IDLE SPEED REVERSE TO DE-CREASE SPEED MORE QUICKLY.

(2) AS TURN IS INITIATED WITH RUDDER HARD TO PORT, IDLE REVERSE IS MAINTAINED TO TAKE ALL FORWARD WAY OFF. REVERSE SPEED MAY BE INCREASED IF BOAT'S WAY IS GOING TO CARRY IT PAST THE TURN AREA.

(3) HELMSMAN WATCHES THE BOW ON THE SHORELINE TO NOTE WHEN THE BOAT STOPS TURNING OR FORWARD MOMENTUM IS LOST. THEN WITH RUDDER STILL HARD OVER, BURSTS OF FORWARD ARE APPLIED, RETURNING THE ENGINE TO NEUTRAL AFTER EACH BURST.

(4) THE TURN IS COMPLETED.

Next try a turn to port as in figure 6. Put the engine in idle reverse and initiate the turn by putting the wheel to port as you coast to a stop. Then give the engine short bursts in forward gear alternating with slow reverse. This will kick the stern to starboard without creating much forward motion.

Once you have learned how the boat reacts in reverse, you can use it to your advantage. If the boat has a right-hand wheel, come alongside a dock at an angle, port side to. When you give it a slight burst in reverse to stop the forward movement, the stern kicks in to port and you end up parallel to the dock at the same time the boat stops.

When cruising under power, engine fuel consumption is greatly dependent upon engine RPM. For good fuel economy and to reduce engine wear, cruise at no higher than about 75% of maximum RPM. For instance, if you put the engine in forward gear after warming up, put maximum throttle to it for a moment and register a top RPM of 2800, then you should cruise at no higher that 2100 RPM. For a displacement cruising sailboat, greater RPM results in only a modest amount of increased speed, yet greatly increased fuel consumption.

GETTING UNDERWAY

Before leaving, it's a good idea to make a last-minute check below the full length of the boat. If you're planning to sail and it's blowing fairly hard, all loose items have to be properly stowed so they can't fall when the boat heels. A bottle that isn't properly stowed could fly to leeward and hurt somebody. The bilge should be pumped dry so bilge water won't slosh up and get into the drawers on the lee side as often happens on shallow draft boats. This should be done while the boat is vertical, because if you think of it after the boat starts heeling most of the water may have already left the sump (the deep part of the bilge) where the bilge water collects for pumping and you'll never get it dry. Even more serious is the chance you may drown out your batteries with salt water, if there's a great deal of bilge water. So make it a habit to pump the bilge dry every time before starting the engine. This also helps you to spot leaks early before they develop into major ones.

Close hatches and portholes. Dog them tight. Portholes on the slanted sides of a dockhouse will be flat (on the windward side) as the boat heels. This can be quite a hazard for crew walking on the deck. They could step right through the porthole and hurt themselves. Recently I failed to "practice what I preach" and accidently stepped through one of these slanted ports right up to my thigh. At least I proved they are dangerous and was lucky not to break my leg.

Also, close any seacocks (the valves that open and close the thru-hull openings to the head, sinks, etc.) where necessary. Some boats have to have certain seacocks closed to avoid flooding when heeled way over. This is a design idiosyncrasy and depends upon the type of boat. If there is a loop in the head, it will keep sea water from getting into the toilet even if the rubber valve that's designed to keep water out fails. If there's no loop, close the seacocks because the valves are not failsafe.

Open the necessary engine seacocks and valves. Many charter companies leave the proper valves open and tell you not to touch them. On the other hand, if the boat has been berthed for a long period of time the charter company may have closed all the seacocks in case the hose leading from one of them springs a leak or pops off causing the boat to sink. It's also a good idea to close the valves leading from the fuel tanks lest a fuel line starts leaking and some spark ignites the fuel. So, before getting underway, it may be necessary to open the salt water intake valve for the engine, the engine exhaust valve and the fuel line valves.

Be sure there's enough fuel. If you run out of diesel, air will get in the system and you will have to "bleed" fresh fuel through the whole fuel system before you can start the engine again. This can take five minutes to an hour depending upon how often you've done it before. Some engines have an automatic bleeding system which saves a lot of work when you run out of fuel. Make sure that the fuel, exhaust, and cooling water intake valves are open before starting the engine.

Next, advance the throttle, make sure the gearshift is in neutral and start the engine. Starting procedures differ with engine types, so we won't get into this.

Check the instruments after you have started the engine. The ammeter should be reading on the plus (+) side to show that the batteries are charging. Oil pressure should read the number of pounds designated in the engine manual, probably about 55–65 pounds. Water temperature should rise to 120–150° F.

You probably are secured to the dock by bow and stern lines and two spring lines. By the way, lest I be taken to task by old salts that we are normally using "piers" and "floats" and not "docks" for pleasure craft, common English usage has made the use of the word "dock" to include piers and floats.

LEAVING THE DOCK

The objective in departing the dock is to do it in a controlled and orderly fashion, leaving little or nothing to chance.

The following docking situations illustrate the techniques for leaving the dock in a controlled manner. In all cases, the last two docklines to be brought onboard are doubled back to the boat. This allows all crew members to be aboard before the boat pulls away from the dock, eliminating potentially dangerous leaps to the departing boat.

Situation 1, figure 7—Double bow and stern lines back to the boat so that the short end of the line is cleated on top of the long end.

The crew releases the bow line and pulls the slack back to the boat. When the bow has blown sufficiently away from the dock retrieve the stern line in the same manner. Put the engine in forward and drive off. Note that the dinghy is tied up short to prevent its painter from becoming tangled in the propeller.

Situation 2, figure 8—Springing the bow out.

Double bow and spring line as shown. Remove all other docklines and place a couple of fenders near the stern. A small amount of reverse will keep the stern against the dock if the wind is shifty.

Release the bow line and use reverse to back the boat against the spring line. This will draw the stern towards dock and force the bow away from the dock.

When the bow is sufficiently off the dock, shift into forward and drive off slowly to allow time for the spring line to be retrieved.

Notice that because the propeller is forward of the rudder and prop wash in reverse is going away from it, turning the rudder will have no effect on the boat while springing the bow out.

Prop walk will be a consideration as the boat pulls away from the dock. When the boat in the diagram shifts into forward, the stern will "walk" to starboard. In this case prop walk is making life easy for the helmsman because the stern walks away from the dock. Had the boat been tied starboard side to and executed the same maneuver, prop walk would be working against the helmsman. If this is the case, simply spring the bow a little further out than otherwise necessary and turn the wheel slightly towards the dock as you engage forward. Prop wash will be deflected to starboard by the rudder and this will mitigate the effect of the prop walk.

Situation 3, figure 9—Springing the stern out

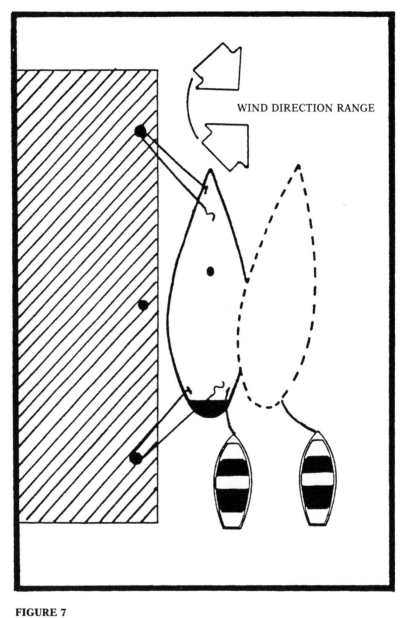

WIND DIRECTION RANGE

FIGURE 7

LEAVING THE DOCK
SITUATION #1

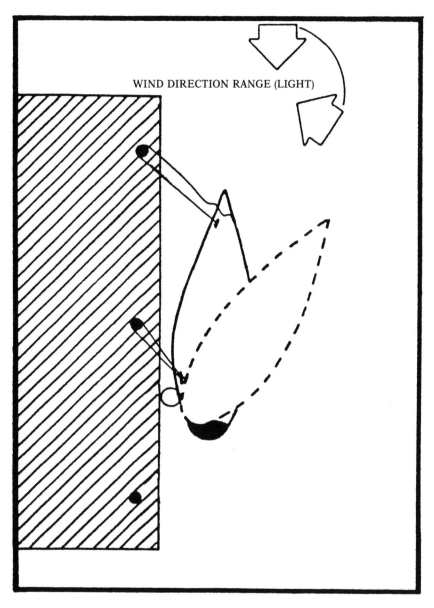

WIND DIRECTION RANGE (LIGHT)

FIGURE 8

LEAVING THE DOCK
SITUATION #2
SPRINGING THE BOW OUT

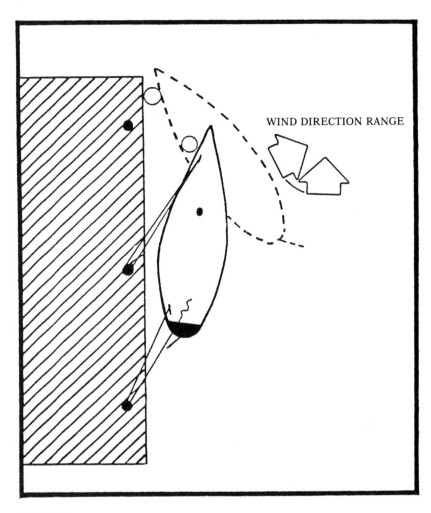

FIGURE 9

LEAVING THE DOCK
SITUATION #3
SPRINGING THE STERN OUT

Again you can use the engine to hold the boat alongside the dock while all but spring line and stern line are removed. This time releasing the stern line with the engine in forward will force the bow in and the stern out. Again, fenders should be placed towards the bow. Turning the wheel hard to port (towards the dock) will cause the rudder to deflect prop wash to port and this will help kick the stern out. When the stern has moved sufficiently away from the dock, power out in reverse as the spring line is brought aboard.

If you want to turn the boat completely around in order to go out in forward gear, use this same system. Have someone on the dock walk the bow along the dock toward where the stern used to be.

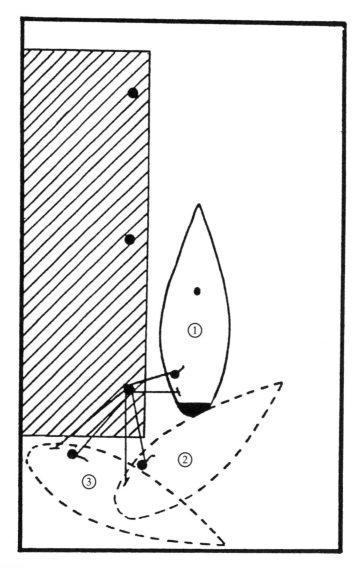

FIGURE 10

LEAVING THE DOCK
SITUATION #4
PIVOTING THE BOAT AROUND THE DOCK

Prop walk will be a factor. In the diagram, as the boat reverses away from the dock, prop walk will bring the stern towards the dock so it is important to account for this when deciding how far to spring the stern out.

Situation 4, figure 10—Pivoting the boat around the dock

1. Reverse boat against doubled spring line. It is important to carefully place your fenders so that the hull won't be damaged against the corner of the dock. 2. Ease the spring line as shown. The boat will pivot more than 90 degrees around the dock. 3. When the bow is pointed in the desired direction engine is shifted to neutral and spring line is retrieved allowing the boat to power off.

Another little trick comes into play if you are secured by docking lines that have spliced loops over dock bitts or pilings. Often other boats' docking lines are on top of yours. Just pull your loop up through inside the other loops, over the top of the bitt, down back through other loops and out. You don't have to take the others off to get yours.

After casting off the lines, make sure none are dangling over the side of the boat where they could tangle in the propeller. Remember how important that engine is to you when you're in a tight spot. It's best to keep the jib sheets in the cockpit rather than on the deck lest someone kick them overboard accidentally. Coil and stow the docking lines and don't forget to stow the fenders. There's nothing more land-lubberly looking than fenders dangling over the side bouncing on waves.

When the wind and/or current is from astern, it may be impossible to leave the dock in forward gear and make the turn away from the dock before running into trouble ahead. The safest departure is often to back away from the slip after springing the stern out as in figure 9. In reverse the propeller is pulling the stern to windward or into the current and the bow just follows. The boat is under complete control. No surprises.

SETTING SAIL

When you're in an open area free of submerged dangers or moored boats, head into the wind to raise your sail. Remember as you are powering out that your salvation if the engine dies is the anchor or your sails. Have them ready to use immediately. The mainsail cover should be off and the halyard attached. The jib should be ready to be unfurled. If space is tight, anchoring is probably safest, but if there's some room to maneuver put your sails up.

To raise sails, slow the engine down to about 800 rpm and try to keep the boat stationary headed right into the wind. If she starts to fall off put her in forward gear and kick her into the wind again. Never change gears unless the engine is practically idling; certainly not if you're over 1000 rpm. Raise the aftermost sail first. If a yawl or ketch, the mizzen or if a sloop, the main. This keeps you headed into the wind like a weathervane. Close any hatches you could fall through if hidden by an unfurled sail. A friend of mine was badly injured when he fell through a hatch that was covered by a loose sail and hidden from view. Take off and stow the sail cover and sail stops. Watch that the mainsail halyard isn't caught forward of a spreader and the leech of the main and the battens don't foul in the shrouds on the way up. The mainsheet should be tended until the leech starts getting tight and then released completely so the sail won't fill the wind before it's all the way up. The cunningham should also be loose and tightened after the sail is up in order to get the stretch out of the lower part of the sail. Make sure the boom vang and the leech reefing lines are free and not inhibiting the sail from being raised. The topping lift should be eased so that the weight of the boom is on the leech of the sail, not on the topping lift, or the sail cannot be trimmed properly. Keep the bow 10 degrees or so off the wind direction. The mainsail will luff to the side keeping the reef lines away from the helmsman and the boom away from the person(s) working on the halyard winch.

Many charter companies have adjusted the topping lift so it doesn't have to be touched. When reefing or furling the mainsail the topping lift holds the boom from falling, but when the mainsail is raised, the topping lift automatically goes slack.

Having raised the main, fall off on the desired tack and cut off the engine IF THERE IS NO DANGER TO LEEWARD! If there are reefs, moored boats or any other potentially dangerous objects to leeward, it's best to keep the engine running until you are well clear. Also, it's good practice to run the engine a total of fifteen minutes to evaporate off any condensation that develops in the first five minutes of running.

Normally, when you charter a boat, the genoa will already be on the headstay, the halyard tensioned and cleated properly and the jib rolled up. Again most charter agencies will ask you not to touch the halyard tension, because they have it where they want it. However, if you charter from a private individual, the jib may have been stuffed in a bag below deck to avoid ultraviolet deterioration from the sun's rays. Or you may have ripped the genoa during the cruise and had the charter company deliver a replacement. In either case the sail needs to be put on the headstay and rolled. First remember how the system works. As the sail is un-rolled, the furling line is rolled up on the drum. As you pull on the jib sheet, and the wind fills the jib, the furling line is wound up around the drum. So when you put a jib up the groove of a bare headstay, the furling drum must be full of line. After taking the genoa out of the bag, find the head of the sail. It's the narrow-est corner. Insert the luff through the pre-feeder and into the groove of the headstay. If there are two grooves side by side and two halyards, use the port halyard with the port groove and the starboard halyard with the starboard groove. Don't cross them. Crossing them creates a chafing situation when you change sails.

Next, follow along the foot of the sail from the tack to the clew to untangle any twists that may have developed. This can be done from the head to the clew along the leech with the same results, but the leech is longer than the foot and checking it consumes more time. The jib sheets should then be tied to the clew with bowlines. Shackles aren't used much anymore on jib sheets be-cause they shake free and can hurt people as the jib flails, as during a tack. The loop made by the bowline should be small, so the clew can be trimmed in close to the jib sheet block (when closehauled) before the knot hits the block. The knot won't go through the block, so if the loop is a big one, the sail won't be trimmed in very tight, particularly if it's a long-footed sail that is cut low. The genoa sheets are usually led outboard of all the shrouds, but that can vary with the type of cruising boat.

Now, pull on the halyard, but watch the tack of the sail and stop pulling as soon as the tack is off the deck. If you pull the jib up too high, it sometimes can jam aloft. Attach the tack of the sail and tension the halyard tight enough to get rid of horizontal wrinkles, but not so tight that deep vertical wrinkles develop.

HALYARD WINCH—USE AND SAFETY

If you are raising the jib while underway, rather then at a dock, attach the tack of the sail first, so the sail can't be lost over the side. Pull directly on the halyard with no turns around the winch until you can't raise the sail any further. Then get one or two turns around the winch and pull directly from the winch, while another crew member "bounces" the halyard (uses their body weight, arms extended, to pull down on the halyard where it exits the mast). If you have too many wraps on the winch you will get overrides. An override is when the halyard going onto the winch crosses over and pinches the halyard leading off the winch, so you can't pull on it anymore. If this happens, you will have to pull all of the turns off the winch and start all over again. When the bouncing slows and you need extra wraps on the winch, pull on the halyard until a foot or so comes off the winch, wrap it around the winch and pull again. Repeat the process until you can no longer pull any halyard off the winch drum. Then, and only then, have a crew member insert the winch handle into the winch. If the winch handle is inserted earlier, you will have to go around the whole winch handle to get the extra turn on the winch. As you "tail" (pull on) the halyard to keep it from slipping, the other crew member cranks on the winch. See figure 11. Most halyard winches have double gears: high when turning the handle in one direction, low when turning the other direction. When you can no longer turn in the high direction, reverse to low. Or rachet back and forth. It's best to pull it in high gear and push in low.

When adequate tension has been applied, cleat the halyard, coil it, and then put the winch handle away. Never leave the handle in the winch as it can get lost and is expensive to replace.

FIGURE 11

WINCHING AND TAILING A HALYARD

When cleating, make one turn around the base of the cleat before starting the standard back and forth crosses. The last loop should be under itself. This is called a "half-hitch" and keeps the line from uncleating accidently. After coiling, the line may be hung by pulling a section of the half-hitch through the center of the coil and over the top of the cleat as in figures 12, 13 and 14.

All lines, and particularly halyards, should be neatly coiled. If a sudden squall hit the boat you need to release the halyards quickly and without the fear that they can get tangled up. Also, the bitter end of each halyard should be secured so that you can just let the halyard go, get on to the next emergency, and know that the halyard won't be lost up the mast. As you coil the line, make the coils clockwise. This will minimize kinking. Always coil from the fast end towards the free end of the line so kinks can be worked off the end rather than trapped. For a right-handed person, hold the line in your left hand leading away from you, run the line through your hand as you stretch out your right arm (the same distance each coil) and then bring it in to your left hand in a loop as in figure 15. When there is a tendency to kink, twist the

FIGURE 12

REACH THROUGH THE CENTER OF THE COIL AND GRAB THE UNDER-NEATH PART OF THE HALF-HITCH.

FIGURE 13

HANG THE COIL ON THAT PART OF THE HALF-HITCH.

FIGURE 14

HOOK THE HALF-HITCH OVER THE TOP OF THE CLEAT. TO RELEASE, JUST
UNHOOK THE HALF-HITCH AND THE COIL IS READY TO RUN.

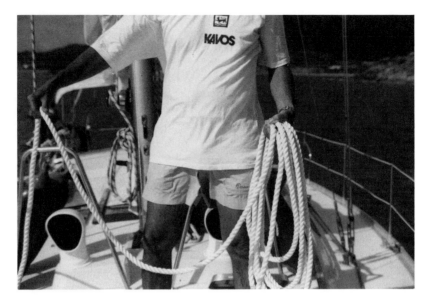

FIGURE 15

USE ONE ARM TO MEASURE THE LOOPS

line clockwise in your fingers. That way kinks disappear off the free end. If the line is long and is terribly kinked, tow it behind the boat and the kinks will disappear. When you are coiling a loose line, such as docking lines, finish the coil off as depicted in figure 16–18 or figure 19–20. Braided lines can be coiled with figure eight loops in the middle and still run freely.

For a halyard that you are finished using but don't have a spot on the mast to secure the shackle, snap it to itself after making an initial loop around the base of a cleat or a railing as in figure 21. Then go back down and secure it.

When underway before unfurling the jib, turn the boat to a reach. Release the line that turns the roller furling drum, but let it out slowly. If you just let go and pull on the jib sheet, the jib will start to unroll slowly. As the wind fills the jib it will unroll extremely fast and spin the line on the drum into a tangled mess that may be hard to use when you want to roll the jib up again. By easing it slowly, with one turn around a winch or cleat so it can't get away, it will roll up evenly on the drum as in figure 22.

FIGURE 16

WRAP THE END OF THE LINE AROUND THE MIDDLE OF THE COILS A FEW
TIMES.

FIGURE 17

PASS A LOOP THROUGH THE MIDDLE OF THE COILS.

FIGURE 18

PASS THE LOOP OVER THE TOP OF THE COILS ON EITHER SIDE AND PULL
TIGHT WITH THE END OF THE LINE.

FIGURE 19

IF YOU'RE HANGING THE LINE, INSTEAD OF PASSING THE LOOP OVER THE
TOP OF THE COILS, PASS THE BITTER END THROUGH THE LOOP.

FIGURE 20

THE RESULT IS EASY TO HANG.

JIB SHEET WINCH—USE AND SAFETY

Tie a stop knot in the end of each genoa sheet as in figure 23. This stop knot is described in our learn to sail book. To trim, put two wraps around the sheet winch. More wraps are added as you pull the sheet in as in figure 24. Use one hand as shown so you can let it slide through your fingers if there's too much strain. Most modern charterboats have self-tailing winches. Just jam the sheet around the top of the winch as shown in figure 25 and crank. Note that the line from the drum must go over the stainless steel guide before being jammed in the black jam cleat. If there are no self-tailing winches, one person will have to pull on the sheet tail while another winches as in figure 26. Remember the line goes around the winch clockwise as you look down on the winch from above. The jib sheets should also be coiled and laid down in the cockpit so the coils run off the top of the coil. If laid down upside down (the coils running off the bottom) the sheet can get tangled. This can be very serious if you had to do a panic tack to avoid a collision and the jib sheet got tangled when it was thrown off the winch. The tangle would keep it from running

FIGURE 21

SECURING A HALYARD AWAY FROM THE MAST: PASS IT UNDER A CLEAT OR
RAILING, BACK UP TO THE HALYARD SHACKLE, THEN TIE THE END DOWN.

FIGURE 22

TYPICAL JIB FURLING DRUM.

FIGURE 23
GENOA SHEET STOPKNOT

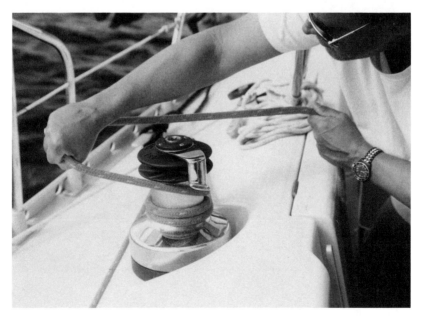

FIGURE 24
THE PROPER WAY TO GET EXTRA WRAPS AROUND THE DRUM OF A WINCH.

FIGURE 25

SELF-TAILING WINCH
MAKE SURE THE LINE PASSES FIRST OVER THE STAINLESS STEEL GUIDE
BEFORE BEING JAMMED IN THE BLACK CLEAT ON TOP.

FIGURE 26

IF THERE'S ENOUGH CREW, IT'S FASTER IF ONE PERSON TAILS. THE
OTHER CRANKS USING BOTH HANDS WITH SHOULDERS RIGHT OVER THE
WINCH.

through the sheet block. As you winch in the jib, watch it to make sure you don't winch too far. I've seen too many people concentrate on the winch with the result that the clew is pulled right into the block or the spreader is poking into the leech of the sail. The trimmer in figure 25 is doing it properly.

When the genoa sheet is eased to adjust to a slight course or wind change, place one hand over the coils on the drum (with your thumb touching your index finger—not sticking out where it can get caught in a loop). Ease the end of the line with the other hand as in figure 27. The hand on the coils controls the speed with which the sheet is eased. Without it, the coils can stick on the drum while the sheet is being eased at the free end and suddenly jerk out, catching you by surprise and possibly pulling your hand into the coils around the winch.

TACKING

As in smaller sailboats there are two basic maneuvers while sailing: tacking and jibing. Since it is a longer process to tack a cruising boat and drains more energy from the crew than on

FIGURE 27

THE PROPER WAY TO EASE A LINE ON A WINCH.

small boats, one tends to be more conservative with tacks. There is a tendency to stay on one tack for a longer period of time and only tack when necessary. Therefore, it is worthwhile to plan the next tack beforehand, not tack indiscriminately only to discover that you then have to tack again to avoid a right-of-way boat, an obstruction such as a moored boat, or to clear a point of land. Assuming that you are closehauled and sailing 45 degrees from the wind, you will tack in about 90 degrees. This means you can sight abeam to windward from the high side of the boat and have a good idea of your heading for the next tack. Make sure that there is no danger in that direction and also look aft to windward for boats that might have the right-of-way on you after you tack. One of the most common errors when tacking a cruising boat is to turn the boat too far. The helmsman usually is used to watching the luff of the jib to determine if he is sailing too high or too low. On a small boat the jib is trimmed in immediately after a tack so he can tell almost instantly whether he has turned the boat too far or not by observing whether the jib is luffing or stalled. On a cruising boat, however, it may take quite a while to winch in the genoa all the way, so all this time it is luffing. The inexperienced helmsman tends to fall off to fill the genoa before it is all the way in. Thus, he has not only turned the boat well past 90 degrees, but also makes it very hard on the crew member who is winching in the genoa which is now full of air. The way to cure this problem is to note your compass heading on the original tack. Then add or subtract 90 degrees depending on which way you're turning the boat. This may sound a bit complicated, but most compasses have 90 degree lubberlines which make it considerably easier. Let's say you are sailing on the starboard tack and heading 100 degrees. Look on the windward side of the compass and note that the starboard lubberline is at 190 degrees (if there's no lubberline, there's usually a screw or some other indication that will suffice). This will be your heading on the port tack after tacking. Remember, this only works if you are closehauled on the original tack. To illustrate by exaggeration, if you were sailing on a beam reach and your heading was 100 degrees, you would end up headed directly into the wind by turning the boat to the 190 degrees in the previous example. So you must test that you are as close to the wind as possible on the original tack before you take your reading. The other caveat to this system is that the wind may shift as you turn. The compass course is only a temporary crutch and must be recognized as such. As soon as the jib is trimmed in, sail by the jib, not the compass until you settle down.

If you are steering a compass course and don't want to sit behind the compass to read it, sit either to windward or leeward and sail by the ninety degree lubberline. It takes a little practice, but it works the same as the forward lubberline, it's just ninety degrees off.

As for the actual mechanics of tacking, the process is a little different with a cruising boat as compared to a smaller sailboat because of the large overlapping genoa. As the boat turns into the wind to tack, the jib sheet has to be released just as a good luff is seen in the jib. If not released early enough, the sail will "back"-fill with wind on the other side—forcing it into the spreader and swinging the bow hard over. Though there is usually no danger involved in this instance, it's hard on the sail to rub against the tip of the spreader under pressure and puts excessive strain on the spreaders. Also, when the sheet is finally released, it takes off with a vengeance and a crew member could get hurt if he got tangled in the sheet as it flew out.

So as the sail starts to luff, the jib sheet person eases the sheet a few feet and then throws the turns off the winch by lifting straight up and flicking them off at the same time. A common mistake is to release at the command "Hard Alee" from the helmsman. Usually, the helmsman gives this command as he starts to turn the boat, which is a bit early for releasing the jib. If the helmsman is late on his or her command, the jib tender must release the sheet before the jib backs. This may make the helmsman upset if not intending to tack. There is one saving factor here; once the jib backs, the helmsman probably can't get the boat back onto the original tack without releasing the jib which is pushing his bow across. So if you aren't positive of the helmsman's intentions, but the boat is turning into the wind, you can't go wrong to release the jib when it's aback. Realize however, that a backed jib is under tremendous load and the jib sheet will zing out fast when released creating a more dangerous situation than a normal tack.

You must be able to release the jib in a hurry in case of a panic or an inadvertent tack. This is not a problem with self-tailing winches. Just unjam the line from the top and flick it off. But if you have a winch that needs the sheet to be cleated on a separate cleat, don't use half hitches, because they tend to be a bit slower to free. As a matter of good practice, take one turn around the cleat base, crisscross cleat in the normal fashion once and then take one last jamming turn around the base of the cleat to keep the line from uncleating.

As the genoa comes across during a tack on a cruising boat quite often the flailing jib sheet catches on a winch, the edge of a hatch, ventilator cowls and other protuberances. It varies from boat to boat and some have no trouble at all, particularly if the crew member takes up on the new sheet fast enough. If the sheet does tend to hang up on your boat, though, a crew member should be stationed forward of the mast to help get the sail and jib sheets across the foredeck. They should be at the middle of the foredeck so they can't get hit by the clew of the sail. The crew member pulls the sail forward along its foot and passes it overhead. Don't stand near the mast where you can be hit by the clew.

The person trimming in the genoa sheet should have one, at the most-two, wraps around the winch to avoid overrides as the slack is pulled in. As soon as there is some pressure, add wraps to avoid losing what has been taken in. There is one fast and safe way of doing this. Take the line in one hand and pass it around the winch two or three times allowing the line to ease through your hand as it goes. Don't ease enough to let the line slip on the drum—just enough to accommodate the extra wraps around the winch. The other hand is used only to feed line to the hand putting the wraps around the winch. I've seen sailors hold onto the line leading from the winch with one hand and make an extra wrap with the other as in figure 28. The result is they are wrapping the former hand into the winch coils and if they don't get it out fast or if the sheet slips out on the drum, that hand can get caught. After sufficient wraps have been taken and the crew member can no longer take in any slack by hand due to the force of the wind in the sail, another crew inserts a winch handle and cranks the sheet in while the first tails (pulls the line) unless you have selftailing winches.

By standing with shoulders over the winch and feet spread for balance, as in figure 26, you should be able to turn the handle continuously in one direction. When you no longer can turn the winch by turning the handle one way, you just change direction of rotation. Watch the genoa as it is being cranked in. If it touches the spreader or the clew hits the jib sheet block you have gone too far. Normally, the faster you can trim the better—or at least the easier. It's much easier to trim the sheet in before the genoa fills with wind, but it's not very efficient. After a tack the boat is going slowly and needs to pick up speed. Full sails (versus flat sails) will help the boat accelerate quickly and a little jib sheet ease makes the sail fuller. So we crank in the last few inches as the boat accelerates. If the sail has filled prematurely, ask the helms-

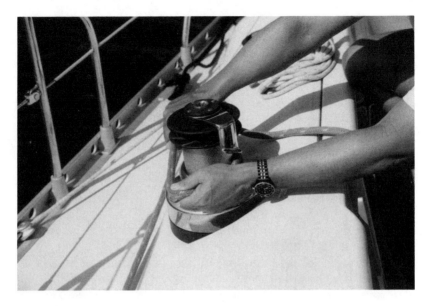

FIGURE 28

THE WRONG WAY TO GET EXTRA WRAPS ON THE DRUM OF A WINCH.

man to head up and luff the sail to make it easier to crank. Be sure to take out the winch handle when you're finished trimming and stow it so it isn't lost overboard.

JIBING

Without a spinnaker set, jibing is a fairly simple procedure. Whereas the main is pretty much forgotten when tacking, when jibing careful control of the main is very important. On a small boat we're concerned with the boom swinging over and beaning somebody, but on a cruising boat where the forces are so much greater, the mainsheet is just as much a threat. If somebody gets tangled in the mainsheet as the boom swings across the boat, they can get hurt quite badly. For this reason, we overhaul the mainsheet as we jibe. This means we trim it in as the boat turns. The bimini tops on most of the Caribbean charter boats keep the boom and mainsheet away from the crew in the cockpit so a jibe is much safer. Still, we trim in the mainsheet to avoid the crash of the boom from one side to the other. As soon as the boom crosses the centerline of the boat (the imaginary line running from the

FIGURE 29

EASING JIB SHEETS TOO FAR WHILE JIBING CAUSES THE JIB TO WRAP
AROUND THE HEADSTAY.

bow to the middle of the stern of the boat) we let the mainsheet out fast.

We first have to release the preventer or the boom vang if it's led to the rail. Then we start trimming on the command "Prepare to Jibe" and when the skipper sees the trimming well underway he or she says "Jibe Ho" and turns the boat. Slightly delay the jibe, because there is no way a crew member can trim in the main as fast as you can turn the boat, except in very light air conditions. In very heavy air often the skipper has to sail the boat slightly by-the-lee to relieve the force on the sail to allow the crew to bring in the main. There should never be a winch handle involved with this type of trimming. Just bring in the sheet hand-over-hand (with one or two turns around the winch so when you ease it out after the jibe you won't get a rope burn on your hands). Under these conditions it's best to center the traveler car and tighten the adjustment lines, so the car doesn't slide across the boat. A sliding traveler car can be dangerous to anyone getting in the way.

The jib takes very little effort when jibing. Just ease the old jib sheet out and pull in the new one. There is only one potential problem: if you ease the old sheet too far the jib will fly out beyond the bow of the boat and when you try to pull it in on the new side the whole sail has to be pulled across the headstay. Note figure 29. The accompanying friction and the flogging of the jib can make this very difficult. So the new sheet should be trimmed as the old one is eased so that the clew of the sail is kept from going too far forward of the mast as the boat jibes.

Chapter 3

RETURNING TO PORT:

ROLLER FURLING GENOA

Most charter companies use roller-furling headsails. In this system, the jib is hoisted in a groove but when not in use, is furled around the headstay, rather than lowered. To furl the sail you simply pull on a line that leads from a drum at the base of the jib aft to a winch near the cockpit, which rotates the whole headstay, rolling up the jib. If you want to reduce sail area, just roll it up halfway. The end result is not perfect because the middle of the stay lags behind the ends in rolling, and the middle of the sail becomes very full. Also, the clew rises higher in the air the more the jib is rolled up. This is fine when reaching in heavy air because there is less chance to scoop water, but it puts the center of effort high off the water and increases heeling. The jib sheet leads will have to be moved to accommodate the new angle made by the jib sheet when the jib is half rolled.

The sail, when rolled up, is still exposed to sunlight and subject to UV deterioration, so sailmakers add a panel of UV-resistant material along the leech. This panel is on the outside of the rolls as the jib is rolled up and protects the rest of the furled sail.

When using a roller-furling system, you generally sail on a reach to unroll the jib. This allows the sail to unroll without flailing against the mast and shrouds. As mentioned before, it's best to control the line from a winch rather that let it fly. If you don't use a winch, when the jib is about half unrolled in a fresh breeze you won't be able to hold the line, and if you just let it fly, the line can become tangled in a turning block or twist and become jammed around the furling drum, making it very difficult to rewind.

To furl the jib, it's necessary to luff it completely. Free the sheet and head the boat up to reduce speed and heel angle, but don't flog the sail against the shrouds. This hurts the sail and increases friction, making the sail more difficult to furl.

If the genoa furling line is hard to pull, DO NOT put it on a winch. First check that the genoa halyard is really tight. To furl well, the luff of the jib needs to be stretched taut, or the furling mechanism won't work well. Excessive headstay sag creates the same problem. Obviously, turning a rod that's curved takes more force than turning a straight one. If there's still resistance, check that the upper furling fitting turns freely. Sometimes another halyard gets wound up in it. Winching can break something. If everything seems clear, but it's still hard to pull the furling line, head downwind and blanket the jib behind the main. Only after you've exhausted other options should you use the winch to furl the genoa. If the jib won't furl at all, something must be broken and the headsail should be lowered to the deck.

After the sail is completely rolled up, roll a couple of extra turns for good measure. Wrapping the jib sheets around the outside of the sail locks the furl in place. There's less chance for the wind to catch some of the sail and unfurl it.

FLAKING MAINSAIL AND SAIL COVER

The mainsail on charter boats is left on the boom from one day to the next. It's difficult to remove it after each sailing session and if the sail is properly flaked down, secured and a sail cover is used, removal is not necessary.

When lowering a main with slides attached to the luff, the slides remain on the mast, piling one on top of the other at the boom as the sail comes down. You flake the sail by starting at the clew and following up the leech, folding the sail over the boom as you go and securing the flaked sail with ties.

An alternative is to make a pocket along the foot of the sail by grabbing the leech 4–5' from the clew, folding the rest of the sail in the pocket (or hammock) formed by this portion of the sail, and rolling it up on top of the boom. Secure it with sail ties, and the sail is furled. This is neater looking if there's no sail cover.

After the sail is flaked or furled and stopped on top of the boom, we protect it with an ultraviolet (UV)-resistant sail cover. First, the cover should be secured around the mast and then stretched aft over the sail along the boom, with the clew end tied tightly. Then fasten the grommet snaps—or shock cord threaded through hooks and eyes—along the edges of the sailcover under the boom, starting at the gooseneck and working aft.

Sail fabric is highly susceptible to the deteriorating effects of the ultraviolet rays of the sun. There is sailcloth and thread available that resist UV rays, but they have not proved totally satisfactory. The only lasting solution so far has been to protect the sails with sailcovers made out of "sunbrella" cloth that filters out almost all such rays, or to remove the sails completely and store them out of the sun, which is often the practice on smaller boats.

DOCKING

The objective in docking the boat is to put the boat alongside the dock so that lines can be secured without risk to the crew members or boat. Preparation is important. The helmsman should have his plan of action clearly defined in his head. This should be discussed with each crew member and specific tasks assigned. All fenders and dock lines should be rigged well before approaching the dock. The approach should be very slow, because, as we have said before, reverse gear on a cruising sailboat is not very effective.

When docking a boat under power, there are only three factors to be concerned about: wind, current, and boatspeed.

If the wind is parallel to the float, it will cause little problem. Given the choice, always approach the float into the wind, because you will be able to control the boat much better with higher engine r.p.m.'s. To slow down, throttle back and the wind will help brake the boat. Approach the dock at an angle between 15 and 45 degrees. As the bow approaches the dock engage reverse which will walk the stern to port more parallel to the dock (if coming in port side to). The bow and forward spring lines should be put ashore first. Once they are secure the boat can be backed against the spring line as in figure 30 until the stern and after spring are secured.

On a downwind approach, to slow down you will have to put the engine in reverse. This gives you far less directional control, and reverse on a sailboat is notoriously ineffective anyway.

Wind affects the boat most when broadside to it. If the wind is blowing across the float, approach with your bow heading almost directly into the wind and turn parallel to the float at the last possible minute. With a righthand prop, the stern will crab to

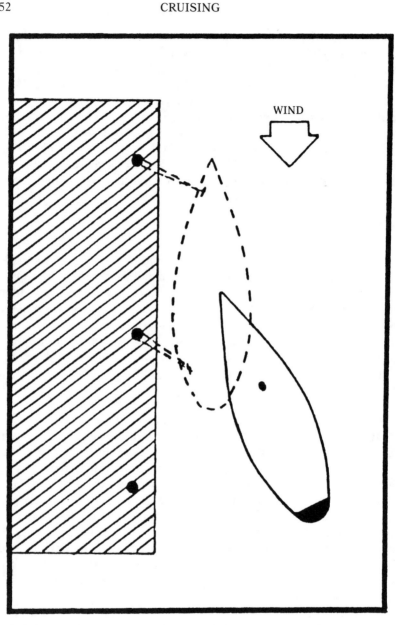

FIGURE 30

DOCKING INTO THE WIND

port when you put the engine in reverse to stop the boat. If your port side is to the float, this will pull you closer, so allow for prop walk in your approach.

When the wind is blowing you down onto the float, it's like coming alongside a float that's a few feet upwind of where it actually is. As you approach, land at an imaginary float upwind of the real one. As your forward speed decreases, you will find yourself making leeway. At a dead stop you should find yourself resting gently alongside the real float.

Current is another friend or foe factor. Used properly, current can be a great friend, helping you to get in and out of tight docking situations. Ignored or used improperly, current can create disaster. Usually you want to approach any dock in an upcurrent direction. That way you can be powering a knot or two through the water and still remain in the same place over the bottom. If you turn the bow a few degrees across the current, the boat will crab sideways and can be fitted into an extremely tight spot between other boats tied alongside a float. This becomes a problem when there's a strong wind blowing with the current. The wind will tend to blow the bow to one side or the other, and when the boat gets across the current—watch out! A solution in this case is to back against the current and the wind. Thus, the engine in reverse is pulling the stern of the boat into the wind and current, so the rest of the boat lines up downwind like a weathervane. Now put the stern a little cross-current and the boat will start to crab right into the docking space or slip.

The third factor in docking a boat is speed. Rarely is trouble caused by too little speed. Sure, you need some boatspeed to be able to maneuver, but if you can't maneuver, it's unlikely you'll hurt much if you're not moving. The big trouble comes from approaching a float or slip too fast. Sailboats build up a lot of momentum that isn't stopped easily and that can damage nearby boats. The slowest possible approach (and departure) is always preferable.

This brings up the same sort of problem: docking in a dead end slip. As the boat approaches the slip, an after spring line and stern line are put ashore at the outer end of the slip, as in figure 31. These lines can be used to stop the boat if the helmsman has misjudged and can't stop the boat in time with reverse.

As mentioned before, preparation for the approach should be completed early. Fenders should be placed over the side. Tie them to the lifelines with a clove hitch backed up by two half hitches. The result looks like figure 32. Too often fenders tied only by clove hitches end up floating behind the boat. Get a bow line, stern line and two spring lines rigged early on the proper side of the boat. One end should be cleated or around a winch, and the line should be led through a chock and back over the lifelines

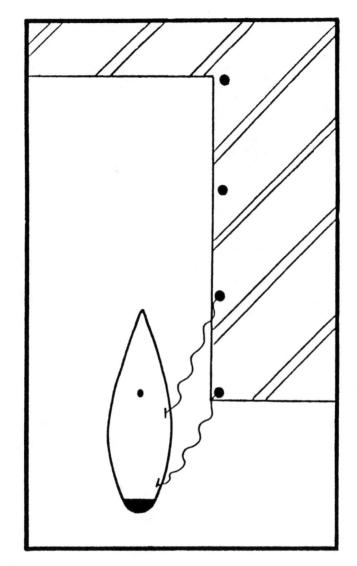

FIGURE 31

DOCKING IN A DEADEND SLIP

preparatory to tossing the end ashore. It's best to have a loop on the end so you can ask a person on the dock to drop it over a bollard or cleat. Then you can adjust the line length from the boat and not have to rely on the person ashore who may not understand what you want.

FIGURE 32

HANGING FENDERS: BACK UP THE CLOVE HITCH WITH TWO HALF-HITCHES.

Of the greatest importance is the spring line that leads from a winch through a chock or block amidships and aft along the float. The chock must be at the center of lateral resistance of the hull, keel and rudder (see figure 33). To find the correct position for the chock or block, attach a line to the toe rail near the middle

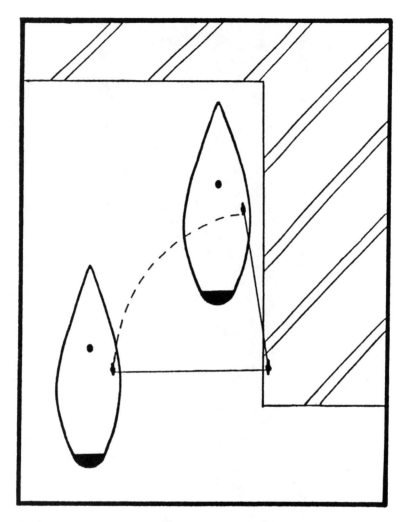

FIGURE 33

A SPRING LINE, PROPERLY PLACED AND PROMPTLY SECURED CAN DO
MORE FOR DOCKING A BOAT THAN ANY AMOUNT OF JOCKEYING UNDER
ENGINE.

of the boat and pull the boat sideways. If the bow comes in more
than the stern, move the block aft until pulling on the line
brings the boat in sidewise parallel to the float.

Set this up as one of your spring lines. As you approach the
float, get that line ashore first and ask the dockhand to drop it
over a cleat or bollard aft near the stern of the boat. A crew mem-

ber should stand ready at the winch to check the forward speed of the boat by easing this line, to avoid crunching the topsides against the float if the boat is moving too fast. As can be seen by the diagram, however, once this line is secured, it describes an arc and any forward motion of the boat brings the whole boat alongside the float parallel to it because of the location of the lead.

The last line to secure is optional—the breast line. This is usually a single line from the middle of the boat to an opposite pier or piling to keep the topsides from rubbing on the float. If you plan to leave the boat unattended for a while, breast the boat a good distance from the float in case of storm. Ease all the lines substantially and take up on the breast line. Then pivot the bow or stern into the float in order to get off and tighten all the lines from the float ends to keep the boat parallel with the float. If you're tying up to a non-floating dock, remember to allow enough slack to accommodate the rise and fall of the tide.

To cut the engine, put it in idle speed, out of gear, and pull the engine cut-off handle. Pull it out hard and hold it out until the engine quits and the engine alarms go on. Then be sure to push it back in and turn off the key to stop the alarms. Sometimes the handle is inadvertently left out. When it comes to start the engine again, it just cranks over, but won't start until some sharp crewmember thinks to check the engine cut-off handle and finds it still out. If you push it in before the engine alarms go off, the engine sometimes starts again. Plus it's a good doublecheck that the alarms are working. Switching off the key then cuts off the alarms.

MOORINGS

In some cruising areas permanent moorings are set out for charter boats to use. This preserves the ecology, because constant anchoring has been destroying coral reefs and the habitat of sea life. Approach the mooring buoy slowly from the downwind side so you are heading directly into the wind towards it. The crew member in the bow should be giving the helmsman directions by pointing at the mooring. Verbal instructions are often hard to hear. Once the pickup buoy or the mooring line has been retrieved, the helmsman must hold the boat in position until the line is secured to the cleat. He puts the engine in neutral unless he sees the crew struggling to pull enough mooring line aboard to secure, in which case he kicks the boat forward for a short time to gain some slack in the line. If the mooring line has a loop in the end, this is placed over the bow cleat. The light line attaching the pickup buoy to the heavy mooring line is then cleated on top of the loop to ensure that the loop doesn't slip off the cleat. The latter could happen if the mooring line were stiff, the loop large, and the bow of the boat pitched down off a wave thereby creating slack in the line. In some cases the mooring has no line. You are expected to use your own. Cleat a dockline on the port bow cleat, pass it through the port bow chock, through the mooring ring and back through the starboard bow chock to the starboard cleat. To leave just release one end.

THE MED-MOOR

As slip space becomes tighter and tighter, maneuvering to enter a slip is becoming more and more of a challenge. The Mediterranean style of mooring stern-to a dock, which permits many more yachts to tie up in an area, was unknown in the U.S. a few years ago, but is now becoming common.

In Greece, the system is to drop your anchor about five boat lengths from the dock and back in. First you must select the spot where you want to end up. If you have come into port early enough in the day, you may find a sufficiently wide open space between two boats to accommodate the beam of your boat without touching the others. That's a rare occurrence in Europe, however, so look for any space you can find between boats. You can usually make the space larger by pushing the others aside. If you see small boats all huddled together rather than intermingled with larger ones, the water in that area may be too shallow for your boat, so be careful. In Europe, more than the U.S., "Might Makes Right," and it's easier for a larger boat to push two smaller boats aside than the other way around.

Having decided where you want to be, maneuver your boat opposite that spot so that your boat is parallel to the others. Drop the anchor about five boatlengths out, or whatever distance seems appropriate for the size of the harbor. We don't go by water depth in this situation. The holding just needs to be good enough to keep your stern from hitting the quay. In many harbors your anchor will hold quite well with short scope because it will catch some of the other anchors and ground tackle if it drags. Also, latecomers often lay their chain anchor rode over yours, thereby increasing your holding power.

Once the anchor is down, the key is coordination between the person on the bow easing out anchor chain and the helmsman who is backing the boat into the space. Steering in reverse takes a bit of practice. Some helmsman like to stand in front of the wheel facing the stern. They can then steer the stern as if they were going forward . . . turn the wheel to the right and the stern goes to the right. This is a very bad habit to get into because your back is to the bow and you can't see what sort of trouble the rest of the boat is getting into. In reverse, the bow makes large swings to either side on a sailboat when the stern moves only a little.

A better position is to stand sideways alongside the wheel, perpendicular to the wheel. When you pull the top of the wheel towards you, the stern comes towards you. When you push the top of the wheel away from you, the stern goes away from you. You can turn your head over one shoulder to look forward and the other to look aft.

A couple of the other persons with "roving fenders"—not secured in place but rather in hand to be placed where needed—are very helpful. The bow person eases a lot of scope in the beginning, so the boat can get some sternway and be maneuvered by the helmsman. If the bow starts falling off one direction or the other, he stops easing, so strain on the anchor will straighten the boat out. Ideally, the anchor chain should be secured early enough so that it takes quite a bit of power in reverse to get the stern near the quay. Lines from either side of the stern are then led to rings on the quay and double back to the boat. As the engine is reversed, take in the slack on one side and then the other. When you're ready to leave you can just throw off the short end of the line and pull it through the ring (less chance of getting a tangle or snags). Finally, put a stern plank to shore for access and egress. Tie it securely to the boat and allow enough overlap ashore so that it doesn't pull over the edge of the quay during the surge experienced in many harbors.

BACKING IN FROM A PRE-SET MOORING

In other parts of the Mediterranean, such as the southern coast of France, rather than drop an anchor and back in, you pick up a preset mooring and back in. You approach in the same manner as above, so that you are prepared to back into the desired spot. If your boat pulls hard to port when you reverse, line it up at an angle as in figure 34 position A. By the time you reach position B

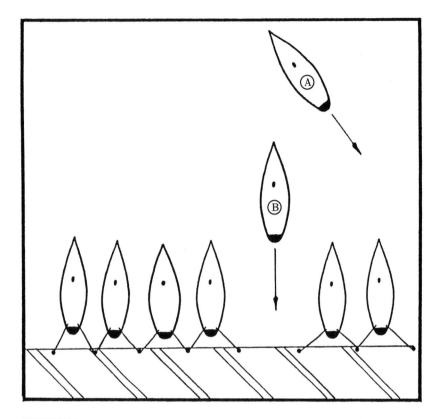

FIGURE 34

STERN-TO DOCKING
REVERSE HARD IN POSITION A AND THROTTLE DOWN IN POSITION B AF-
TER WAY IN REVERSE HAS BEEN ESTABLISHED.

the boat has some momentum in reverse, you are lined up with
the slip and can reduce power. With steady, low RPM's the boat
will back in a straight line. Most problems develop when skippers
race the motor in forward, reverse, forward and reverse again.

With a boat hook you either pick up a bow line attached to the
mooring or pass your own line through an eye in the mooring
buoy and back to the boat so you can ease back, as you wish. At
the same time, lift up the messenger line that leads from the
mooring to the quay so a crew member on the stern can reach it
and can guide the boat backwards. Often the mooring buoy is
eliminated leaving just a messenger from the bow mooring line to
the shore. When almost docked, you follow the messenger line to
the mooring line and secure it to your bow. The messenger line

can be messy with seaweed and growth, so I prefer to let it run over the boathook out over the side of the boat rather than bring it aboard. Thus the helmsman must rely less on the messenger line and more on skill, so it depends a bit on the experience of the helmsman as to how much you rely on the messenger line to aid in the maneuver.

Because each boat has her own mooring and does not need to drop an anchor, this system is obviously less chaotic than the other on both arrival and departure. Although it saves far more space than the U.S. system of docking alongside, it is predicated on the beamiest boat. When a number of narrow boats are using adjacent moorings, there's usually excess space left between them. A common solution to this is a combination of the two systems. Instead of dropping anchors, a mooring system is used, but without messenger lines ashore. The moorings are placed quite close together, so even narrow boats can squeeze next to each other and have their own mooring.

ANCHORING

It's always important for a skipper to know the characteristics and capability of his ground tackle and anchor, especially when in charge of a boat other than his own, as when chartering. Over the years of exposure to numerous charter agencies we have observed how the emphasis of the charter checkout we have been given by each charter agency has changed. Initially the emphasis was on the mechanical systems on the boat and on navigation. Anchoring was covered in passing. As years of charter checkout progressed, anchoring became more and more emphasized, probably because poor anchoring procedures had caused more problems than anything else. Anchoring problems often occur in the middle of the night when the crew trying to cope with them is half asleep and possibly slightly under the weather.

When choosing a place to anchor in a crowded anchorage drop your anchor almost alongside (slightly aft of) another boat of like characteristics that will be affected by wind and current somewhat comparable to your boat. After letting out comparable scope, no matter what direction you swing, you will not touch, as in figure 35. By being slightly aft you can get your anchor up in the morning even if his position has changed to dead ahead of your boat.

Even if you find your anchor directly under another boat, don't get upset. Just power up very close to the other boat, take in all

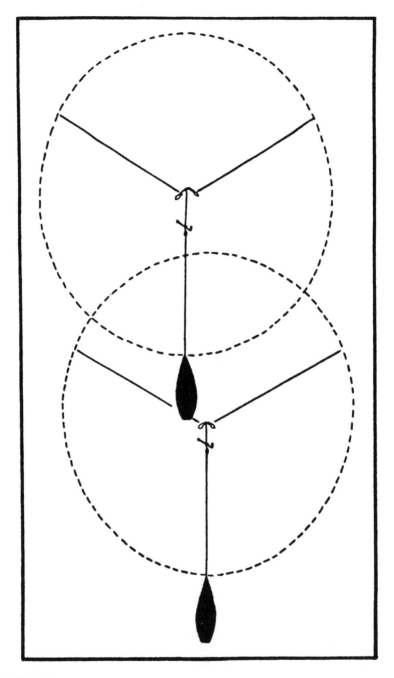

FIGURE 35

DROP ANCHOR NEAR STERN OF ANCHORED BOAT. AS BOTH BOATS SWING THEY CAN'T HIT.

the slack in the anchor line and reverse your engine. Since the anchor line is almost vertical, scope will be almost nonexistent and the anchor will easily drag out from under the other boat.

If a 360 degree anchor light is required by the rules, be sure to put one on your bow about six feet above the stemhead fitting. It's required unless you are anchoring in a "special anchorage" area designated by the Coast Guard and shown on the nautical chart.

In very protected waters with only a light breeze on a hot summer's night, consider anchoring from the stern, so the stern will head into the wind. This allows the light breeze to come down the companionway and any aft opening hatches to cool off the sleeping area. The best way to accomplish this is to anchor the normal way from the bow. Then snap a snatch block over the anchor line with a line back to the jib sheet winch or through a turning block on the stern to a jib sheet winch. Pulling on this line will bring the anchor line to the stern outside of all the standing rigging and lifelines. After the boat has been turned around with the stern towards the wind, cleat off the anchor line. This way the anchor has not been uncleated from the bow and if an unexpected squall comes through in the middle of the night, all you have to do is unkleat the stern and ease the snatchblock line for the bow to swing back into the wind. The last thing you want in the dark during a squall is to try to detach an anchor line from the stern and re-attach it to the bow.

As for an anchor's holding power, the major variables are the type of anchor and its weight, the angle the anchor line makes with the bottom, and the type of bottom. Some common anchors are shown in figure 36. A Danforth anchor holds well in a muddy, rocky bottom, but poorly when the bottom is grassy (covered with seaweed). A plow anchor is better at grabbing on a grassy bottom. The best bottom for anchoring is hard sand. A yachtsman's anchor has to be heavy to be effective and is awkward to handle. The Bruce anchor has yet to become popular in the U.S. It is probably the most effective all-around anchor of all. The heavier the anchor of any type, the better the holding power.

The smaller the angle the line makes with the bottom, the better the holding. If the line is almost vertical, the anchor will lift rather that dig in. However, if the line is almost horizontal, the anchor will dig in hard. The most common method to reduce this angle is to let out more line or "scope". A four-to-one scope is enough for temporary anchoring such as a lunch stop, but a six-to-one or seven-to-one scope is recommended if you want to sleep well at night and not worry about dragging. This means to let out

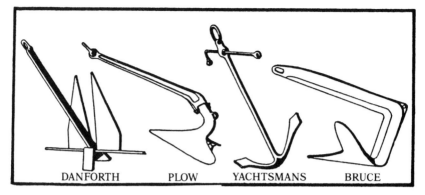

DANFORTH   PLOW   YACHTSMANS   BRUCE

FIGURE 36
POPULAR TYPES OF ANCHORS

anchor line equal to seven times the depth of the water you're anchoring in, and be sure to consider the tide factor and the height of your topsides as well. In Long Island Sound, for instance, if you anchor in eight feet of water at low tide and let out 60 feet of anchor line (7:1), you are only going to have a little over 3:1 scope when a six-foot tide and four feet of topsides brings the effective depth up to 18 feet. Also, you may have anchored at slack tide with little current. When the current starts to flow fast, you may start to drag.

Use your depth sounder to determine water depth where you're anchoring—15 feet, for example. Add the expected rise of tide— say, 5 feet and your height off the water (4 feet) for a total of 24 feet. Multiply the result by six and let out 144 feet of scope. Until you are well aware of how much line this represents, it might be useful to place colored plastic markers along the line at 20 foot intervals.

Another way to increase holding power by reducing the angle the anchor line makes with the bottom is to drop a weight along the line on a messenger called a "sentinel". Snap a snatch block on the line with the weight attached and lower it 20 feet or so. This has an added advantage of making the line from the bow to the weight more vertical than before and reduces the risk of the anchor line wrapping around the keel.

The pin of the shackle that connects the anchor rode to the anchor can sometimes work loose resulting in the loss of the anchor. To preclude this possibility, use seizing wire to keep the pin from turning.

Some cruising skippers set out two anchors at 45 degree angles off the bow. This helps reduce swinging when there is limited room in an anchorage, but does not add much to holding power. The holding power is the square of the weight of the anchor or of the two anchors combined. Square a 12 lb. anchor and you have 144. Square an 8 lb. anchor and you have 64. Two 8 lb. anchors give you a holding power of 128, still not up to that of the single 12 lb. anchor. However, the foregoing doesn't take into account that if one anchor drags, there's still another to save the boat.

Furthermore, if the current changes and you're using a single Danforth anchor, it's possible for it to flip over and not dig in the other way either because of weed or a stone wedged between the shank and a fluke. With two anchors out at approximately 45 degrees either side of the bow, the greatest angle either one can rotate on the bottom is 90 degrees. Each anchor, once set, will just rotate rather than pull out, and will be reset as the boat passes over it with the current.

The best way to set two anchors across the wind is relatively simple. Choose your anchoring spot, drop one anchor and pay out anchor line over the windward side of the boat while powering directly across the wind. It's better to power rather than sail. Head the bow 10 to 15 degrees into the wind to offset leeway and to adjust for apparent wind. Predetermine the amount of line that will be used and cleat it at that point before you make your run. For instance, if the depth is 20' and you decided on 140' of line, get both anchors ready, each with 140' of line flaked on deck and cleated. When the end of the first anchor line is reached, drop the second anchor and pay out its line. You will end up solidly anchored by the two anchors and able to absorb all sorts of wind and current changes without excessive swinging.

Adding a length of chain between the anchor and line will also increase holding power; the chain then must be lifted before the anchor is affected.

When anchoring in areas where the water is very deep, such as the Society Islands of Tahiti, a combination of chain and nylon line works quite well. An anchor rode made up of 60' of chain and 300' of nylon seems to be a good answer for anchoring in 70' to 90' of water every night. The chain increases holding power and resists the abrasion of coral heads, and the rope reduces the weight of the whole arrangement. One drawback is that when weighing anchor, the transition of the rope to chain on the windlass can be difficult because you have to switch from the rope drum on the windlass to the chain drum. If I were asked to vote on the chain/line controversy, I would have to cast my vote for a combination such as the above. In shallow water the rode would be all chain. As the wind increased and you added scope, you'd gain the advantages of line. I would also have aboard a smaller anchor with an all-line rode for lunch stops and for protected-water anchorages with a mud or sand bottom which wouldn't snare and chafe the line.

There are other areas, such as Turkey, where the bottom goes out from the shore at a shallow gradient for a few hundred feet and then drops off steeply to a depth of 100–150 feet. The standard system is to anchor in the shallow water and then take a line ashore to a tree. Floating lines are much easier to use for this purpose and less likely to get wrapped around the prop. Thus, if the anchor drags at all, it will drag into shallower water thereby increasing the holding power. Without a line ashore, the anchor could drag towards the deep water and in the middle of the night you might discover yourselves drifting around the harbor with the anchor dangling off the bow in deep water.

One other way of increasing holding power that appears to be quite effective is "backing an anchor"—have two anchors in a series, with one attached to the other in line by a short piece of chain. Thus, even if one pulls out, the other is set. This is rarely used, but if you expect a storm and don't have two long anchor rodes, tie two short rodes together into a long one and back the anchors. It will hold far better than two anchors on two short rodes.

When approaching your selected anchorage, have your anchor ready on deck. If the anchor line is stowed in the forepeak, make sure plenty of it has been pulled out on deck so that the anchor will reach the bottom without pulling more line out of the hawsehole (the hole in the deck leading into the forepeak anchor line storage area). The line, of course, should have been carefully stowed in the first place. If a tangle develops under the deck, it's a nasty mess to handle in an area that's hard to reach. Make sure, however, that the bitter end of the anchor line is secured, either in the forepeak or on deck, before the anchor is put over. Then, after the boat has come to a complete stop, lower the anchor into the water gently until some of the weight is reduced by water pressure and then let go.

After the anchor is down, let the wind blow the boat downwind. We see a lot of impatient skippers who can't seem to relax and let the boat settle back. They have to gun the boat in reverse which makes it difficult and dangerous for the person in the bow letting out scope. Plus the anchor starts dragging before there's enough scope out. Be patient. Make sure a crew member has snubbed the dinghy in close so the painter can't get under the boat and wrap in the propeller. Ease out scope as she goes, and when you have let out all your intended line, snub the line around a cleat so that the momentum of the boat will set the anchor. On a sailboat with a fine bow and high topsides, the bow blows way off to leeward. It may blow so far that the stern ends up upwind of the bow. In that case, if the engine is in reverse, put it in neutral and, rather than wait until the boat finally lines up with the wind again, power in forward gear downwind to set the anchor. Watch that you don't run over the anchor line and wrap it in your prop.

When enough scope is out, put the engine in neutral. As the anchor sets, the bow will turn towards the anchor (upwind). If you steer downwind in the opposite direction and the bow still turns upwind towards the anchor, you can rest assured the anchor is well set. Now, either leave the engine in neutral and let the wind blow your stern around or use the engine in reverse.

As you drop back, the bow person should apply gradually increasing pressure on the anchor line. When the anchor has been set, secure the line, reverse the engine and test it. You can tell whether or not it's dragging by grasping the line beyond the bow; the vibration will be transmitted through the line to your hand. If it becomes obvious that you are ending up too close to another boat that was there first, raise your anchor and try again. The courtesy is, "He who anchors last, moves first."

Next, take compass bearings on nearby landmarks or lights so you can check later on to determine whether or not you've dragged the anchor. There are three caveats to this advice. If the landmark is nearby, the normal swinging on the anchor will radically change the bearing and you may think you are dragging when you aren't. If the landmark is far away, you will have to drag a long distance before there is a bearing change. If the visibility deteriorates you can't see the landmark, so bearings have limited value.

On one cruise our flotilla of chartered sailboats anchored close together near some reefs. In the middle of the night, I woke up to find us bumping against the bow of a companion boat. Rain was driving down and visibility was only a few feet. Our impulse was to get the anchor up immediately and move to another spot. We took up enough scope to stop bumping and started the engine, but I told the crew not to get underway until I plotted a safe course. The wind direction had completely reversed and had we headed in the direction we had previously been oriented, we would have ended up on a reef. When you are disoriented, sleepy, and have a problem to face, try not to do anything rash. Take the time to plot a safe course, decide on how many minutes to run that course, turn on your running lights and trust your compass. It's the best friend you have.

On another cruise in Tortola, we tried to anchor in a harbor on Jost Van Dyke in the British Virgin Islands. It was late in the afternoon and the anchorage was crowded. The wind was blowing onshore, so we rounded the sterns of the anchored boats and headed out between them to drop our hook. It was clear that we would be unable to drop the anchor and drift backwards without fouling one of the boats on either side, because we couldn't track in a straight line until there was enough scope out to take a bite with the anchor without dragging. So we chose to go upwind of the fleet, power straight downwind through the fleet, drop the anchor over our bow between two of the anchored boats, and when there was enough scope out so that we were behind the other anchored boats (but not too close to shore), we snubbed the anchor line. The anchor grabbed and spun us around 180 degrees, right in the spot we wanted to be for the night.

The crucial part of this maneuver is to put the engine in neutral as you drop the anchor and pay out the line fast lest it get caught around the prop. Also, the anchor line should be flaked on deck so it can pay out quickly without snagging, and the bitter end must be cleated. You must be powering at a good clip when you drop the anchor, so you'll continue in a straight line when you put the engine in neutral. It's a system that's rarely called for, but under special circumstances, it's one that really works. If you are concerned about dropping the anchor from the bow because of the chance of fouling your prop, take your anchor and line to the stern. Power slowly downwind and drop the anchor where you want to place it. You have complete control and can power between other closely anchored boats. Also, since you don't have to put your engine in neutral, you can power more slowly, which makes it easier and safer to pay out scope. When you reach your desired location, snub and cleat as before and, when securely anchored, take the end of the anchor line up to the bow (outside all stanchions and shrouds) and cleat it. Then release the line at the stern. This method, though taking more effort and preparation, is a surer and safer method of anchoring in a crowded anchorage.

Occasionally, before putting the anchor over you may wish to attach a tripline, a light line attached to the anchor's crown that will pull it out backward, in case it is snagged. A small buoy attached to the tripline will float directly above the submerged anchor. This also gives the skipper a mark to head for in order to get the boat right over the anchor before raising it.

To raise the anchor, start the engine and motor toward it. A crew member on the bow should be pointing toward the anchor position as the line is gathered in, because the helmsman will not be able to see the direction of the line. Hand signals work best here as in figure 37. Voice communication may be lost in the noise of the engine. When an anchor windlass is being used, the person overhauling the line off the windlass should hold it low, so it doesn't come off the top. Also, when you are pulling on the line, the coils tend to ride up to the top of many windlasses and will tend to override or tangle. The way to keep the coils from tangling is to stop pulling for a second or two and let the coils slip on the windlass. They will drop down into position and you can pull again until the coils ride up to the top. When the anchor line is vertical, the crew signals to the helmsman to put the engine in neutral and snubs the anchor line. The forward momentum of the boat will break the anchor out. The engine should be in neutral and the boat at a complete stop as the anchor is raised. Forward motion bangs the anchor against the bow.

If the anchor doesn't break out as the boat rides over it, the crew should cleat the line and the helmsman puts the engine in

FIGURE 37

HAND SIGNALS HELP THE HELMSMAN KNOW WHICH WAY TO TURN TO PLACE THE BOW DIRECTLY OVER THE ANCHOR. BY THE WAY, WORKING WITH THE ANCHOR ON BARE FEET CAN BE DANGEROUS AND IS NOT RECOMMENDED.

forward gear and hits the throttle in an attempt to break the anchor out. If at first unsuccessful, he can then try different angles. In heavy seas, try an alternative method: when the bow goes down, take up slack in the anchor line and snub it. As the bow rises on the next wave, the boat's buoyancy may break the anchor free. The slack may have to be taken in on a series of waves before the line is vertical enough for the maneuver to work. If this system doesn't work, lead the anchor line back to a jib sheet winch and try to winch it up. Failing this, don your mask and flippers to look the situation over for a solution.

If, after looking the situation over, you decide the anchor line is wrapped around a coral head, ease out 60 feet or so of anchor line and power with the helm hard over heading the bow to the outside of the circle. This allows the boat to circle around the snag with a constant outward pull on the line, but keeps the line from wrapping around the keel. To reverse the direction of rotation, reverse the engine until the boat and anchor are in line, turn the wheel so reversing puts the bow to the other side of the anchor, then power forward with the wheel hard over; i.e., for counterclockwise circling, the helm is hard to starboard in forward gear and vice versa for clockwise circling, as in figure 38. This should unwrap the line if you can see which way it's wrapped. If you can't see, circle in both directions. If there's no "give" or loosening in one direction after two or three circles, go four to six circles in the opposite direction. The nice thing about this method is that you are putting great outward pressure on the line. The boat will be almost parallel to the line and will be pulling every degree of the circle rather that just a few angles—as is the case when the bow is vertically over the fouled anchor and you power forward in a few directions.

If your anchor has caught on the anchor line of another boat, as in figure 39, you will find it very difficult to unhook the line with a boathook once your anchor is out of the water. Cleat about 10 feet of spare line to the bow cleat, pass the free end under the other anchor line (or the other anchor as in figure 39) and cleat it. Lower your anchor so it unhooks the other line and then bring your anchor all the way up. Next uncleat one end of the spare line and let the other anchor line drop. It's a simple, safe and easy procedure.

During the night with two anchors set, the boat sometimes does 360 degree turns and both lines end up wrapped around each other. Instead of trying to pull them apart on deck, which just tightens the wrap the further down the lines you get, work on

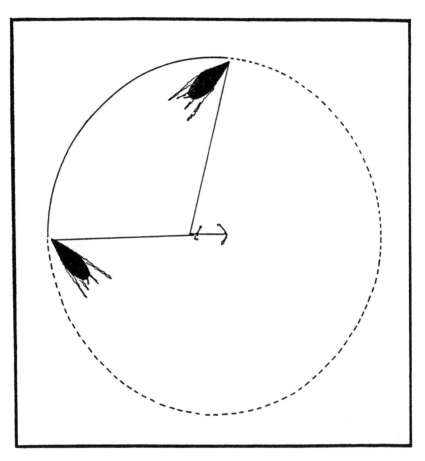

FIGURE 38

HELM TO PORT TO GENERATE THE OUTWARD PULL WHILE CIRCLING CLOCKWISE.

just one line. As you pull it in, make big loops on the other line and then drop the loops down the tight line. After the first is raised it's easy to get the second one up.

The same vagaries of wind and tide in the middle of the night may wrap your single anchor line around the keel of the boat, so you end up anchored by the keel of your boat when it comes to raising the anchor in the morning. Tie a fender or floating cushion to the end of the anchor line and drop the whole thing over the side. Send someone in the water to loosen the wraps around the keel allowing the anchor line to drop off. Then just pick up

FIGURE 39

HOOKED ANCHOR: PASS A LINE UNDER IT, LOWER YOURS TO UNHOOK THE
ANCHOR, RAISE YOURS AND SECURE IT, THEN RELEASE THE PREVIOUSLY
HOOKED ANCHOR.

the fender and line under power. One warning: BE SURE the anchor line is well secured to the fender or cushion. If you use a bowline, back it up with a couple of half-hitches. Bowlines can and do untie by themselves when floating around in water. Also, don't put the engine in gear until the swimmer is back aboard the boat.

Some people raise their mainsail before raising their anchor. If you have a broken engine, this is necessary. However, if you are doing it just to save time and you intend to power up to your anchor, it can be a major source of problems. If you snub the anchor when the line is vertical, power in forward to break it out and the anchor sticks, for instance, the boat will pivot across the wind or even downwind. Now the mainsail is full and you may be heading at another nearby anchored boat when suddenly the anchor releases. Believe me, it's better to get the anchor up and stowed while under engine, and then power to open water in order to raise the mainsail.

When the anchor eventually breaks the surface, clean the mud off before bringing it aboard and then make sure it is well lashed down on deck before setting sail.

THE DINGHY

Charter agencies try to use dinghies that are light enough to be easily handled, yet large and stable enough to handle most of the charter party in one trip ashore. Thus all dinghies are a compromise. Loading the dinghy has to be done carefully. One person steps in at a time, into the center of the boat and sits down before the next person gets in. Usually a ladder will be put over the side of the sailboat and the dinghy brought alongside. The dinghy will be rising and falling in swells, so wait until it's at it's highest position before you step in. If you go too far down the ladder and try to step in when the dinghy is rising, not only can it throw you off balance, the edge of the dinghy can hit your foot on the ladder and give you a nasty bruise.

When there are waves breaking on the shore, don't dinghy all the way to shore. Get out of the dinghy just short of the surf and either anchor the dinghy there or guide it in. Pull it well up the beach and anchor it, or tie it to a tree lest the tide comes in and sweeps it away while you're gone.

Don't swim after a dinghy that is drifting away. With any amount of wind, the dinghy will probably drift faster than you can swim. Recently there was a drowning a few miles from our home for this very reason. If you're on your anchored sailboat, quickly tie a fender to your anchor line and throw the whole thing overboard. Tie it well or you may lose your anchor and the complete anchor rode. After you've retrieved the dinghy, you just pick up the fender. This is much faster and less hassle than raising the anchor.

More dinghies are lost at cocktail parties than at any other time. You row over to the host boat to find several other dinghies hanging off the stern. I recommend tying your dinghy to a stanchion with a bowline rather than cleating it with all the others. Often there are two or three dinghy painters on the same cleat and the first person to leave the party uncleats the others to free his painter and then recleats them with one hand while holding his own painter in the other. After a few drinks he occasionally misses a painter or two—possibly yours. When you come to get your dinghy darkness has fallen and—surprise—the dinghy is nowhere to be seen. If you're cruising in the Caribbean, it's somewhere between your harbor and Central America. Lots of luck finding it.

Avoid the problem: tie it with a bowline; tie it separately; tie it yourself.

When you leave a mooring, anchorage or other congested area, your dinghy is snubbed in close to the boat until you get your sails up and are sailing. This is to avoid wrapping the dinghy painter around your propeller. Now you want to let the painter out, but there's a lot of strain on the line. First tie the bitter end of the line to a stanchion with a bowline, so no matter what happens you can't lose the dinghy completely. Then uncleat the line leaving a 360 degree loop around the base before the crisscrosses. Then ease the line. The friction of the loop should make it easy to hold on to even with the dinghy being pulled at speed. When the proper scope is out, cleat it. Leave the bowline on the stanchion. It doesn't do any harm and might come in helpful.

When you tow your dinghy in any seas, it's a good idea to double up on the towlines. Use one as a primary painter and another as a safety line tied to another fitting on the dinghy and led to a different cleat on the boat. Either take the oarlocks, oars and outboard off the dinghy or make sure they are well secured. The former is the best policy. Tow the dinghy aft of the sailboat on the back of about the third wave astern so the dinghy rides bow up rather than scooting down the face of the wave.

In bad sea conditions or on a long passage, particularly at night, don't tow the dinghy at all lest it swamp and break the towline. Rather, hoist it aboard with the main halyard and a three-part bridle attached to the bow and two corners of the dinghy transom. Then lash it upside-down on the cabin top or foredeck. That should be a one- or two-person job, and you will rest a lot easier knowing your dinghy is secure.

Chapter 4

SAIL TRIM

Having covered the basic maneuvers, setting and dousing sail, and docking/mooring procedures, let's look a little closer at the sails the second time out.

We covered very thoroughly the use of jib telltales in our *"Colgate's Basic Sailing,"* the text for our basic course. Only a short review is needed here since their use on cruising boats is just the same as on smaller boats. We place wool along the luff of the sail at three levels. The helmsman should be able to see the lower level from his position. Appropriate levels are $1/4$, $1/2$ and $3/4$ of the way up the luff and about 8" to 12" back from the headstay for a 30' to 40' cruising boat. Many people add additional telltales, because the more information you have about the flow over the leeward side of the sail, the better. If the windward ones flutter you are too high or the sail is eased too far. If the leeward ones flutter, you are sailing too low or the sail is trimmed too flat. It's as simple as that. If the upper windward telltales flutter before the lower windward ones do, then your jib lead is too far aft. If the lower windward ones flutter before the upper ones do, the jib lead is too far forward.

SAIL CONSTRUCTION

But first, just a bit about how a sail is constructed. The threads that run across a strip of sailcloth are called filling threads, otherwise known as the "weft" or the "fill". The threads that run lengthwise are called the "warp". Warp stretches more than fill, but the greatest stretch comes in a diagonal direction, called the "bias". Most sails are designed with this stretch in mind.

For example, the mainsheet will exert the greatest force on a mainsail and most of it will fall on the leech. Consequently, the panels of cloth are sewn together so that the crosswise threads, or filling threads, lie along the leech of the sail.

This means that all the panels of the luff along the mast are cut on the bias, where stretch is greatest. Note figure 40. If we were to blow up a small section of the sail along the mast (figure 41) we would see that the threads look like a whole bunch of little diamonds on the bias. As we pull down on the luff and increase the tension, each diamond elongates (the dotted lines in figure 42) and pulls material in from the center of the sail.

If we pull down hard on the luff when there is not enough wind to warrant it, vertical troughs or creases will appear that run parallel to the mast. You can simulate this effect by taking a handkerchief and pulling it at two diagonally opposite corners. The same troughs will appear just as they will when there is too much tension.

There are two ways to tension a mainsail's luff: with a downhaul (that pulls the sliding gooseneck lower) and a cunningham. In the days of cotton sails you would buy a sail that was actually too small in light air. This would allow you to stretch it to the legal size limits when the wind velocity increased. Of course this meant you would automatically penalize yourself in light air by having a reduced sail area. To solve this dilemma, Briggs Cunningham, skipper of *Columbia*, winner of the 1958 America's Cup, chose the simple expedient of placing a grommet above the tack fitting and, when the tack reached down to the black band on the mast (and had been stretched as far as it could be legally), a block and tackle arrangement was attached to a line running through the grommet. When it was tightened it would add more tension to the luff, and legally so.

Some wrinkles do appear along the tack below the grommet when the cunningham is in use, but they don't seem to make an appreciable difference in the efficiency of the sail. So just forget them.

This grommeted hole in the mainsail has become known as a "cunningham hole" and it is now common-place in most classes of sailboats. With a cunningham a sail can be made full size for light air performance, and still be tensioned along the luff to keep the draft from moving aft when the wind increases.

Luff tension must also be changed depending upon what point of sail the boat is on. When reaching or running you want a very full sail with the draft well aft. You should ease off the downhaul and cunningham in this situation.

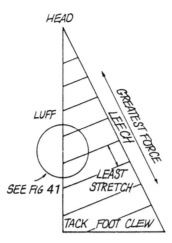

FIGURE 40

MAINSAIL PANELS LAID SO LEAST STRETCH IS ALONG THE LEECH.

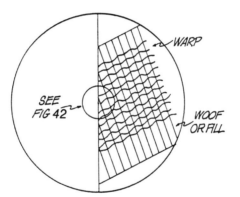

FIGURE 41

THIS PANEL LAYOUT MEANS THE BIAS IS ALONG THE MAST

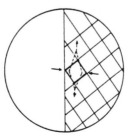

FIGURE 42

STRETCHING THE LUFF PULLS MATERIAL IN FROM MIDDLE OF THE SAIL TOWARDS THE LUFF.

Actually, you don't really have to be concerned with this high level of efficiency, unless you are racing. But you should always remember that inadequate jib luff tension, with its accompanying "scallops," immediately brands the skipper as a slovenly one.

APPARENT WIND

Apparent wind direction and velocity changes due to changes in boat speed are also well described in the chapter entitled "Sails and Wind" in our basic manual. However, certain ramifications of the effect of a change in true wind velocity on the apparent wind direction and velocity were left out as being too advanced for the novice sailor to comprehend. We have redrawn the diagram so you can follow it here, figure 43.

The dot-dash line shows the resulting change in apparent wind if the true wind suddenly dies. With boat speed remaining constant and the wind velocity lowering to six knots, the apparent wind will go forward. One way to remember this is to imagine the wind dying completely just as though someone had switched off a giant fan. Obviously, in the absence of any wind, the only breeze you would feel would be that produced by the forward motion of the boat and would come from dead ahead. So any reduction in true wind velocity must bring the apparent wind forward.

This happens quite often on light days, particularly to large cruising boats that have a great deal of momentum. The sails will start luffing and give the appearance of sailing too high or too close on the wind. Actually the boat is only traveling through a light spot or "hole" in the wind. The helmsman must make an immediate decision: is it a valid wind shift, called a header, or is it just a hole? If it is the former, he must head off to fill the sails. If it is the latter, he could kill what little speed he has by heading off instead of shooting through the light spot with momentum and picking up the breeze on the other side.

It's always a difficult decision to make unless you can see a puff ahead. Usually the wisest course is to head off very slowly and evenly. If you're still luffing after turning 20 degrees away from the wind it's probably a flat spot.

One warning. A skipper who reacts precipitously and turns the boat quickly downwind actually aggravates the situation if it's just a hole in the wind. The turn itself forces air against the lee side of the jib causing it to luff or back. In a short time he will find himself 30 degrees below his previous course, but the jib is

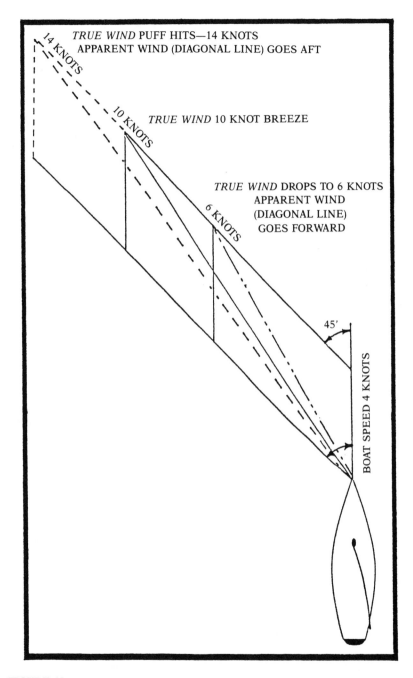

FIGURE 43

WHEN THE TRUE WIND DIES THE APPARENT WIND GOES FORWARD.

still luffing because of the turning movement of the boat. Of course it may not be a hole, but rather a true header (the wind shifts towards the bow). The boat is sailing a straight course in a light, steady breeze and suddenly, because of the wind shift toward the bow of the boat, the jib starts to luff.

The skipper decides that instead of heading off to fill the sails, he will tack. As he turns the bow into the wind, the jib will fill as the apparent wind comes aft, due to the turning of the boat. Because the jib has stopped luffing, it can appear that the wind has shifted back to its original direction. The skipper can have the impression that he has been lifted (the wind direction has changed more toward the stern of the boat) when actually it is only the pivoting of the boat that has caused the change.

An inexperienced or indecisive skipper will stop his tack in the middle and return to his original course. At first it will appear that he has made the correct decision because, by making the incomplete tack, he has slowed the boat which puts the apparent wind fairly well aft. As the boat picks up speed the apparent wind will again come forward and he will find himself still sailing in the same header he had before.

Now let's consider other cases where wind speed remains constant but boat speed varies. For instance, if the boat starts surfing down the face of a wave (much as the surfboarder would use a wave) the apparent wind goes forward. Sometimes it goes forward to the point where it will flatten a spinnaker back against the mast and rigging! At other times the boat may slow down for some reason. The apparent wind comes aft and its velocity will increase. As the wind velocity doubles, the pressure on the sails and rigging quadruples.

When a boat runs hard aground at high speed it is often dismasted because the rig and sails have a tendency to keep on going even though the hull has stopped. But another important reason is the apparent wind pressure on the sails has increased suddenly.

A good example of this happened to *Mare Nostrum*, a 72' yawl, on the 1955 Transatlantic Race from Cuba to Spain. We had a spinnaker, mainsail, mizzen and a mizzen staysail (sort of a jib for the mizzen mast) set in fairly fresh winds of about 20–23 knots.

The swivel on the spinnaker halyard broke and the chute went streaming out ahead of the boat. Before we could get it aboard, it filled with water, went underneath the bow, and hooked on the keel. This slowed the boat down so suddenly that the top half of the mizzen mast toppled forward under the increased load on the mizzen staysail. So always remember that whenever there is a change in either boat speed or direction or wind velocity or its direction, there must also be a change in the apparent wind. A helmsman must be alert to it and either change his course accordingly or the crew must trim or ease the sails.

SAIL SHAPE

Poor sail shape and trim can increase heeling. Heeling is undesirable for a number of reasons. When a boat heels, the bow digs in and the center of effort of the sails falls outboard, rather than directly over the center of lateral resistance of the hull, causing a strong weather helm—a tendency for the boat to round up into the wind when the helm is released. The pressure on the helm needed to keep the boat sailing straight creates rudder drag and slows the boat down. When heeling, the sails do not expose as much area to the wind as in figure 44. With less "lateral plane", the keel will be less effective in preventing leeway and the boat will slip sideways more. Moreover, once the rail buries in the water, turbulence from the cap rail, stanchions, turnbuckles, sheets and other fittings greatly increases the drag and slows the boat. Lastly, it's less comfortable to be on your ear all the time particularly if you're trying to cook. Of course you can reduce heeling by reefing, but if you reef too early you sacrifice speed. Some very simple things can be done to improve your sail shape to reduce weather helm and heeling, yet improve speed.

A common problem with older dacron sails is the movement of the draft as the material stretches and gets "tired". It's also a problem for new dacron sails as the breeze freshens. The sail cloth stretches and the draft moves aft towards the leech. Basically, the draft is the maximum depth of the sail at any given cross section (figure 45A), and is usually expressed as a percentage of the chord (the distance in a straight line from luff to leech). The normal position of the draft in a mainsail is 50 to 55 percent aft from the luff and 30 to 35 percent for a jib. Figure 45B shows a mainsail where the draft has moved aft toward the leech. The resulting shape, with battens cocked to windward, forces the airflow to exit to windward on the weather side and to separate into turbulence on the lee side of the sail. Such a shape, with its stalled airflow, will create a strong weather helm and a great deal of heeling. Stretch the luff of the sail tight by increasing halyard or cunningham tension to counteract the movement of the draft aft in the sail.

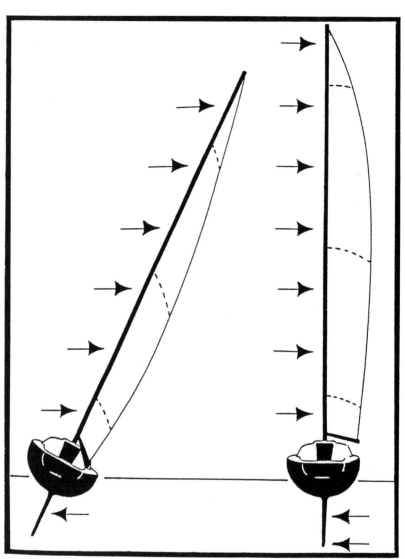

FIGURE 44

AS THE FORCE OF THE WIND HEELS THE BOAT, THE SAILS PRODUCE LESS
DRIVING FORCE, THE KEEL PRESENTS LESS LATERAL PLANE AND THE
ADDITIONAL WETTED SURFACE INCREASES DRAG. THE RESULT: REDUCED
BOAT SPEED AND MORE LEEWAY.

On light days, the draft in the mainsail may move aft and
causes a tight leech because of excessive mainsheet tension when
sailing to windward. Be careful not to trim the mainsheet too

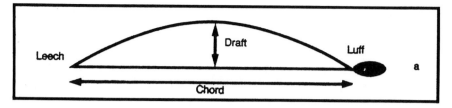

FIGURE 45(A)

DRAFT IS THE MAXIMUM DEPTH OF THE SAIL AT ANY GIVEN CROSS SEC-
TION AND IS EXPRESSED AS A PERCENTAGE OF THE CHORD.

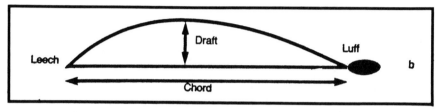

FIGURE 45(B)

IN THIS MAINSAIL, THE DRAFT HAS MOVED AFT TOWARD THE LEECH, CRE-
ATING WEATHER HELM AND INDUCING UNDESIRABLE HEELING. TO MOVE
DRAFT FORWARD, TIGHTEN THE HALYARD TO STRETCH THE LUFF.

hard. This can be avoided by moving the traveler to windward,
which allows you to trim the boom to the centerline of the boat
with less downward pull (see figure 46).

On very light days, the weight of the boom can cause the battens to cock to windward. Tightening the boom topping-lift and
taking the weight of the boom off the leech of the sail can solve
the problem. Ideally, when sailing to windward, if you sight up
the mainsail from beneath the boom, the second batten from the
head should run parallel to the boom in almost any wind condition. Note the tight leech in figure 47A. The battens cock to windward. By reducing mainsheet tension, the battens start to line up
with the boom (figure 47B).

Lack of leech tension is almost as detrimental as too much
except in heavy winds. This usually occurs when reaching. The
boom is out over the water and the wind force on the sail causes
the boom to lift. The upper part of the sail can actually be luffing
even though the bottom part is full of air. This effect is called
twist and it is usually undesirable.

There are a couple of exceptions. The wind on the surface of
the water is slowed down by friction, so the wind at the top of the

FIGURE 46

MOST CRUISING BOATS HAVE EASILY ADJUSTED TRAVELERS AS ABOVE. JUST RELEASE THE LEEWARD SIDE AND PULL THE TRAVELER TO WIND- WARD ON LIGHT DAYS. THIS ALLOWS THE BOOM TO BE IN THE CENTER OF THE BOAT WHEN SAILING TO WINDWARD WITHOUT OVERTRIMMING THE MAINSHEET.

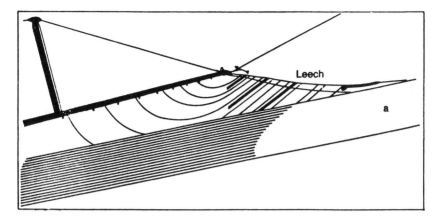

FIGURE 47(A)

TOO-TIGHT LEECH TENSION IN THE MAINSAIL CAUSES BATTENS TO COCK
TO WINDWARD.

FIGURE 47(B)

EASE THE MAINSHEET UNTIL THE SECOND BATTEN (FROM THE TOP)
LINES UP WITH THE BOOM.

mast has a greater velocity than at the deck. Thus, the top of the
sail is sailing in a continual puff relative to the bottom of the sail.
The apparent wind comes aft in a puff. And in order for the ap-

parent wind to have the same angle to the luff all the way up and down, a slight twist at the head of the sail is necessary.

The other exception to the harmful effects of twist is when there is very heavy air. The upper part of the sail greatly affects a boat's heeling just as the weight at the top of the mast does. If you want to reduce heeling, simply reduce the effectiveness of the upper part of the sail by inducing twist. Instead of easing the traveler out, ease the mainsheet.

When the mainsheet is eased the battens fall off to leeward and the driving force is greatly reduced. Under moderate conditions, you should drop the traveler car to leeward and tension the mainsheet to reduce twist. This will work until the boom passes the end of the traveler. Then the key is good boom vang tension.

The boom vang is a block and tackle device that is used to reduce the twist in the mainsail (figure 48). It pulls the boom down when you are reaching or running and, in doing so, keeps the leech from falling off to leeward. This means that the same angle of attack of the apparent wind to the chord will be maintained along the full height of the sail, thus making the sail a

FIGURE 48

SELF-CLEATING BOOM VANG LED TO BASE OF MAST. CAN BE UNSNAPPED AND LED TO THE RAIL FOR MORE DOWNWARD PURCHASE OR TO HELP PREVENT ACCIDENTAL JIBES.

much more effective airfoil. On some cruising boats, the boom vang has to be taken off every time the boat is jibed and set up on the other side once the boom is across. Don't forget to remove it when you jibe. When the wind fills the other side of the mainsail and tries to force the boom across against the restraining boom vang, something has to give if it's blowing hard. The boom vang may break, the boom may break, or, if neither happens, the boat may broach out of control. Compare figure 49 with figure 50. Notice how the leech has tightened and the sail shape has improved by using the boom vang.

When running, lack of vang tension can enhance rolling. It's obviously uncomfortable, though not necessarily slow, to be rolling wildly from side to side. Some of it is caused by the top part of the sail falling off to leeward because the boom has raised up in the air. The head of the mainsail may actually line up with the wind direction and pick up attached airflow, resulting in drive in a windward direction (figure 51A). As the mast rolls to windward, the apparent wind goes forward and airflow is attached farther down the sail adding to the drive to windward. Each roll makes the situation worse. By pulling down hard on the vang, twist (the difference between the angle of the sail to the wind at the top compared to cross sections further down) is reduced and the drive is in a more forward direction (figure 51B). If rolling persists, trim the main boom in a little and harden up to more of a reach.

Draft in a jib should be farther forward than in the main. A stretched out, baggy jib with the draft well aft will make your boat feel extremely sluggish and tender. You'll heel badly and sail slowly from the drag of the baggy leech. The slower a boat sails, the less effective the underwater surfaces are at reducing leeway, so the whole thing is cumulative. Use strong halyard tension to keep the draft in a forward position. Slide your jib fairleads aft and use less jib sheet tension if the leech is cupped in too tight or the wind is heavy. A problem signal is too much backwind in the mainsail from the jib. A little backwind is fine, but when the sail burbles to windward in moderate winds, the shape of the jib needs work.

THE BOOM PREVENTER

This is the name given to a line running from the end of the main boom forward to a cleat near the bow. If you are running dead downwind in rough seas on a cruising boat for a long period

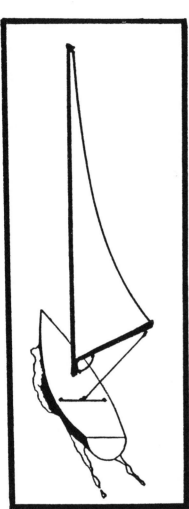

FIGURE 49

SAIL TWIST DUE TO INADEQUATE LEECH TENSION CAN BE REMEDIED BY DROPPING THE TRAVELER TO LEEWARD AND TENSIONING THE MAINSHEET.

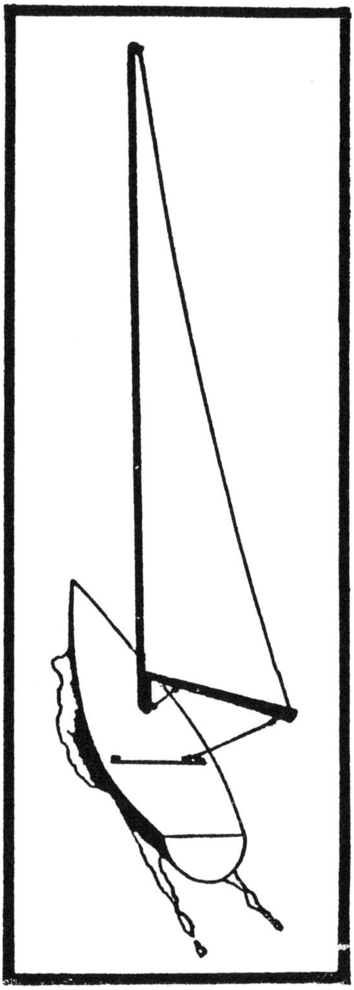

FIGURE 50

WHEN REACHING OR RUNNING, A BOOM VANG WILL TIGHTEN THE LEECH, REDUCE TWIST AND IMPROVE SAIL SHAPE.

of time, there is always the chance of an accidental jibe. Such a jibe could wipe out some unsuspecting crew member. The line to the bow is long enough so that if the wind fills the other side of the main, the line will just stretch rather than breaking and allow the helmsman the opportunity to get back to course. The boom

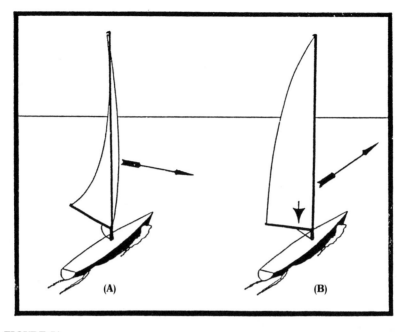

FIGURE 51

(A) WHEN RUNNING, SEVERE MAINSAIL TWIST CAN CREATE DRIVE IN A
WINDWARD DIRECTION.
(B) BY TIGHTENING THE VANG, TWIST IS REDUCED AND DRIVE IS IN A
FORWARD DIRECTION.

preventer is often used at night and on long downwind passages, but is too complicated to set up for a short run. On short runs, it is up to the helmsman to keep the boat from sailing "by-the-lee" and for the crew to always be aware that at any time during a run the boom could come swinging across due to helmsman error. An alternative is to unsnap the boom vang from its connection at the base of the mast and snap it to the rail as far forward as possible. Then pull it tight for a combination vang and preventer.

PROPER JIB ADJUSTMENT

As we described earlier, twist in the mainsail is the falling off to leeward of the top part of the sail from inadequate leech tension. The same problem exists with the jib, but it is the fore and aft placement of the jib lead (the block that the jib sheets run through) that determines how much twist a jib will have.

If the lead is too far aft, the jib sheet will pull along the foot of the sail, but there won't be enough downward tension on the leech. The result is that the top part of the sail will tend to luff first. However, other things can have the same effect as moving the jib lead block forward or aft. For instance, if the mast is raked (leaned) aft by lengthening the jibstay it effectively moves the lead aft as the clew is lowered.

A good thing to remember is that the opening or slot between the jib leech and the body of the mainsail should remain parallel. This means that if we induce twist in the mainsail in heavy weather to reduce drive in the upper part of the main and thereby reduce heeling, we also must do the same thing to the jib.

Conversely, in light air, any fullness should be down low in the jib. You can accomplish this by easing the jib sheet, which has the same effect as easing the outhaul on the main along the boom. Easing the jib sheet increases draft by shortening the distance between the tack and the clew, and this gives you greater drive in light airs and lumpy seas. However, there is one detrimental side effect to easing the jib sheet: it frees the leech. As the clew goes out, the angle of the jib sheet is lowered. Therefore, to regain the proper leech tension using less jib sheet tension, you must move the jib lead forward.

One usually increases the tension on the luff of the sail to control the jib's shape as the wind increases. As the jib stretches under the force of the increased wind velocity the draft tends to move aft in the sail, and more luff tension is required to keep the draft in the same location.

But if the luff tension is increased by tightening the jib halyard, the clew rises in the air as a result, and the lead will need to be placed further aft. In heavy air you may even want a little twist in the sail, and the lead may need to come back a bit further.

However, if you get your luff tension by pulling down the luff downhaul or jib cunningham, the clew will be lowered and the lead will appear to be aft of its previous location. Since it is blowing relatively hard when this is done, you may not want to change the jib lead position, for it is now effectively aft of where it had been. This may produce the desired twist.

As a boat falls off onto a reach, the jib sheet is eased and a great deal of twist can develop. In order to correct this, the lead must go forward again. In the old days sailboats did not have effective boom vangs for their mains and the top part of the mainsail twisted off to leeward when reaching. In order to make the jib leech match the curve of the main, sailors would move the jib lead aft.

Not so, today. Effective boom vangs keep twist in the main to a minimum and, therefore, little twist is needed in the jib. So in most cases the lead, when on a reach, should go forward not aft, to pull down on the leech and reduce twist.

SAILING WING & WING

Since a cruising boat has a very large jib in comparison to most smaller boats, it behooves us to make use of it at all times. When sailing downwind, it is blanketed by the mainsail. The mainsail is catching all the wind and none is getting to the genoa. The only way we can make the genoa "draw" (fill with wind) is to cross it over to the other side of the boat, where the wind is passing unobstructed. This is called sailing wing and wing. The mainsail does help, because it changes the direction of the wind that hits it. Notice in figure 52 that the masthead fly (the wind indicator at the top of the mast) shows the wind almost directly behind the boat—that's the backstay you see in the photograph. However, the flags on the port speader clearly show the wind coming from the starboard side. So the wind is hitting the mainsail and spilling around the mast at an angle. It's obviously effective to wing a jib out to that side and catch the force from the wind off the main before it's lost.

On larger cruising boats in light air, this bending effect often isn't enough to keep the genoa full. The genoa is so long on the foot that the weight of the clew folds the leech in and collapses the sail. It keeps coming into the middle of the boat rather than staying where it should. By sailing quite far "by-the-lee" the jib will stay full, but this can cause an unscheduled jibe. The solution is to wing out the genoa on the spinnaker pole. First, attach the spinnaker pole topping-lift to the pole. One person lifts the pole with the topping-lift and another guides it. Remember, we are talking about a boat the size of a 35–45 foot cruising boat. One much larger or smaller might use slightly different techniques. Next, attach one end of the pole over the windward jib sheet. That's the sheet on the side of the boat opposite the side the main boom is being carried on, not the literal side the wind is on. For example, if you're sailing "by-the-lee" the wind is coming over the same side as the main boom, but it's still called the leeward side of the boat. Then, keeping the pole level with the topping-lift, push the pole straight forward and place the other end of the pole in the eye or socket designed for it on the mast.

FIGURE 52

THOUGH MASTHEAD FLY INDICATES WIND DIRECTLY AFT, FLAGS SHOW
THE FLOW OFF THE MAIN WHICH HELPS WHEN SAILING WING AND WING.

Lastly, release the leeward jib sheet and pull on the weather one. The clew will first go forward to the pole as you take the slack and then, when it hits the pole it will start to pull the pole aft. In most cases you can pull the pole right aft until it touches the shrouds, particularly if the genoa is a large one and you're sailing well downwind. It's a good idea to rig a boom preventer when sailing wing and wing. You'll be quite surprised at how much this increases your speed.

This technique is also used on racing boats when it is blowing too hard to set a spinnaker. When cruising, some boats lower the main and set two genoas out on twin poles to either side of the boat. The two jibs have more sail area than the main and jib together and tend to pull the boat along downwind so that it barely has to be steered. This system is unavailable on most bareboat charters.

When sailing wing and wing you must anticipate right of way situations very early. For instance, if you are on port tack with your jib winged, you have to keep clear of all boats on starboard tack. If you are caught by surprise and have to fall off sharply, the mainsail will jibe and the boat will broach (heel way over). The spinnaker pole will be digging deep into the water as the boat heels and it is entirely possible that the pole will break as it is pressed back against the lee shrouds. If you turn the other way, harden up, the winged out jib will back (the wind will get on the other side of it) and force your bow back down in the direction you were trying to avoid—right into the right-of-way boat. Try it in medium breezes. Wing out a jib on a pole and then try to tack. It's very unlikely you'll be able to tack unless the jib is a tiny one. So anticipate the right-of-way boat early to negate the need for a sharp maneuver at the last moment to avoid it. Watch the right of way boat very carefully as it approaches. If the bearing doesn't change you had better make a course change for collision avoidance.

To take the pole down and get the jib over to the normal side you must take all the pressure off the sail. Therefore, ease the windward jib sheet. This will allow the pole to come forward to the headstay and the genoa to fly out in front of the boat. Remember to steer the boat downwind. You don't want to change the course until the pole is completely off and the jib is in its normal position. Next, unsnap the windward sheet from the jaws of the pole and lower the topping-lift so that the end of the pole rests in the bow with both jib sheets over it. Then trim in the leeward jib sheet to get the jib back to its normal position preparatory to hardening up. Last, take the pole off, stow it, and unsnap and secure the topping-lift. When the pole is stowed, make sure it isn't on top of a jib sheet.

SHORTENING SAIL

It's common practice on cruising boats to reduce the sail area when the wind velocity increases to the point where the boat is "overpowered". This means the boat is heeling so much that its speed has decreased.

The normal progression for shortening sail on a cruising boat is to reef the main first, then if the wind increases, change to a smaller jib. With still more wind, reef the main some more and, if that isn't enough, go to an even smaller jib. The object is to re-duce sail equally between the main and jib to keep the boat well balanced. You can take the main down completely and sail under small jib alone if you are reaching or running. If beating to wind-ward, however, to douse the main completely is a good way to lose a mast. The mainsail absorbs a great deal of shock when the boat pounds through a wave. As it hits the wave, the mast whips forward and then aft. The presence of a mainsail, even reefed, reduces the whipping. I remember sailing a particularly windy Block Island Race a number of years ago on a 53' yawl. The owner claimed the boat was unbeatable to windward in a blow with a #2 jib and no mainsail. He was proving his point as we were nearing the finish in the lead that night when the headstay turnbuckle parted from the strain and we had to retire from the race. A number of dismastings in recent years have been attrib-uted to sailing without a mainsail. In one St. Petersburg to Ft. Lauderdale race I sailed, the wind was a steady 35 knots on the nose (a beat, in other words). The Gulf Stream was against the wind causing quite a steep chop—ten to twelve feet high. We were down to a small genoa staysail and the main was reefed as far as we reasonably could. The professional hand on the boat insisted we douse the main and I equally strongly insisted we don't. I won out and when we arrived in Ft. Lauderdale and looked over the boat in daylight the next day we found two wires had pulled out of the swaged fitting that forms the eye for the turnbuckle jaw on the starboard after lower shroud. We were on starboard tack and as the middle of the mast bowed forward after the boat "fell" off the top of one after another of those waves and hit the bottom of the trough, the after lower shroud and the mainsail were the only two things keeping the mast from bowing farther. If we had lowered the main, we would have certainly lost that lower shroud and would have lost the mast.

The standard method of reefing a mainsail is called "jiffy reefing" or "slab reefing"—take your pick. A line runs from an eye on the boom up through a grommet hole in the leech of the sail a few feet up, back down around a pulley at the end of the boom and forward to a winch near the gooseneck. See close-up figure 53. A similar grommet hole is located a few feet up the luff of the sail above a hook welded to the gooseneck. To reef: 1. Ease the mainsheet. 2. Lower the halyard (figure 54). 3. Hook the luff grommet on the hook. You may have to take the lower slides out of the groove of the mast. 4. Tighten the halyard (figure 55). 5. Winch the leech line in tight (figures 56 and 57). You may have to ease the boom vang and mainsheet to get it tight. 6. Secure a safety line through the leech grommet and around the boom. 7. Trim in the mainsheet and the sail is reefed. The excess material along the foot is just disregarded or tied in with reef points. This is an extremely fast reef to make and is very popular on modern charter boats. The order is extremely important. Complete the forward part of the sail first before touching the leech reef line. If you start winching in the leech reef line before the new tack is hooked or the halyard is tight, you will cause yourself all sorts of problems. To shake out the reef, do

FIGURE 53

REEFING HOOKS AT THE GOOSENECK. NOTE REEFING LINES EXITING OVER TOGGLE CLAMPS SO THE LINE CAN BE TAKEN OFF THE WINCH (OUT OF PHOTO JUST UNDER "DANGER" SIGN).

FIGURE 54

LOWER HALYARD FAR ENOUGH TO HOOK THE LUFF GROMMET ON THE REEFING HOOK.

FIGURE 55

AFTER HOOKING, TIGHTEN HALYARD SO LUFF IS VERY TIGHT.

FIGURE 56

THE LEECH REEFING LINES BEFORE REEFING.

FIGURE 57

WINCH THE LEECH REEFING LINE VERY TIGHT SO HORIZONTAL WRIN-
KLES SHOW ALONG THE FOOT. MAINSHEET AND VANG MUST BE LOOSE.
THIS IS DONE AFTER THE REEF OF THE LUFF IS FINISHED AND THE HAL-
YARD TIGHT.

all the foregoing steps in reverse order. If you don't untie the reef points before easing the leech reefing line, you will rip the sail at the reef points.

When reefing tighten up the main halyard extremely tight. There is a tremendous amount of pull on the head of the sail transmitted along the leech from the mainsheet tension. When the head is near the top of the mast the halyard pull angle is almost opposite the leech pull angle (see figure 58), but when reefed most of the leech pull is against the upper slides. That's why the slides near the head of the mainsail on a cruising boat are usually doubled up and sewn on with special care. The strain on them can be eased by very tight halyard tension. If you don't tighten the halyard you may very well rip off the upper slides, particularly if you are beating which is the point of sailing that produces the most mainsheet pull on the leech of the sail.

The other half of shortening sail is to roll up the roller furling jib. Roll it far enough to keep the boat well balanced. Gusts of wind shouldn't blow the bow off to leeward. If there's a second jib, a fore staysail, to the middle of the foredeck, use it instead of the genoa when the wind gets over 30 knots. It's an excellent heavy weather sail.

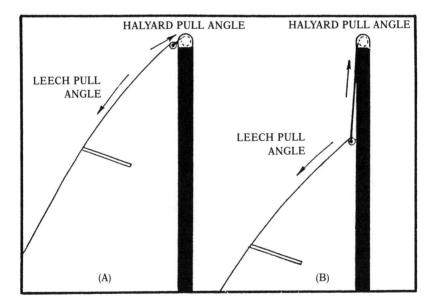

FIGURE 58

(A) UNREEFED, LEECH PULL IS OPPOSITE THE MAIN HALYARD
(B) REEFED, LEECH PULLS LUFF AWAY FROM MAST AND HALYARD HAS TO BE HIGHLY TENSIONED TO COUNTERACT IT.

Chapter 5

SAFETY & HEALTH TIPS

Sailing is one of the safest sports there is, but as the wind and sea build up, the visibility decreases, navigation problems develop, and parts of the boat start to fall apart (like a short in the electrical system, a broken boom, ripped sails or a leak developing) one begins to wonder just how safe it is. The problem is you can't just cry "Uncle—I've had enough, let me off". You have to cope and often have to head further offshore until the wind subsides because of the dangers near shore you're unable to see. It's doubly hard when you know there's a nice snug harbor back there you'd love to be in, but don't dare approach.

Most charter areas are in protected waters, but in some spots, like Greece, you have 50–60 mile stretches of open water. Here are some safety and health tips that might make your life easier if caught in a storm: CREW—Have enough crew members aboard. There should be at least two people on deck at all times. When the going is very bad I've found, even on boats with experienced crews, that often 50% of the crew will be seasick and essentially helpless. With an inexperienced crew, there may be only one or two out of six or seven crew members who are not sick. This is a disaster for the healthy ones if the storm lasts a couple of days. So not only must you have adequate numbers of crew, you must be sure of a nucleus of crew members you can depend on in any sort of blow.

When sailors suggest that a seasick victim stay on deck where he can see the horizon and breath fresh air, they know what they're talking about. Another tip: Let the queasy person steer. It often helps to be doing something active that necessitates looking up at the horizon. Steering also provides anticipation of what the next movement of the boat will be, which can be helpful.

Among the other causes of seasickness, what you eat is high on the list. If you drink too much alcohol the night before sailing, you will be more prone to getting sick. If you eat greasy, hard-to-digest foods, you also increase your chances of getting sick. Some of the first signs of the onset of seasickness are burping and indigestion. I recommend eating saltines and drinking Coke or Pepsi. These two drinks help reduce the chances of getting sick because they contain phosphoric acid, which is an ingredient in Emetrol, a drug to control vomiting. That's the medical explanation I received from a doctor when I asked the reason why a Coke seems to settle the stomach.

There are other seasickness cures—some good, some not so good. One of the "nots", in my estimation, is ginger root. This has been a traditional cure for queasiness for centuries, and may be effective for some people in mild sea conditions. I bought some ginger root pills and offered them to a number of Offshore Sailing School graduates on our Tahiti cruise. The passage from Bora Bora to Raiatea was a beat in reasonably brisk winds and steep seas. Those that tried the ginger root pills, all swore "never again". Not only were they sick, they were burping ginger, which made them feel worse.

One of the good remedies for some people is a product called Sea Bands. There's a pressure point on your wrist three finger thicknesses from the bend of the wrist and between the two tendons that, when pressed, seems to reduce queasiness. To make this work you have to press both wrists at the proper point. Sea Bands are simply elastic wrist bands with a button on each to put pressure at the proper spot. A similar product, Accu-Band, uses a velcro wrist band to press the button on the wrist. The Chinese discovered this and call it acupressure. We have found that it works for quite a few people, and since there are no drugs or side effects, the bands are ideal for health-conscious sailors.

While we're on the subject of acupressure, you may not think that hiccups are much of a problem, but for some people they can be. I was working with a television anchorman following some races in a motorboat. He suddenly wanted to go ashore because of bad hiccups. The last time he suffered hiccups he had them for three days, until every hiccup was extremely painful and he had to be operated on at a hospital to stop them. The acupressure point for hiccups is exactly where the wedding ring is worn (on both hands). Just press with your thumb and forefinger on the top and bottom of the patient's ring finger at that point on both hands until the hiccups stop. It worked right away with the TV anchorman and I've worked it many times before and after.

As for seasickness drugs, Scopolamine behind the ear patches, which can be obtained only with a prescription, work well for many people. There can be side effects such as drowsiness, dry mouth and in some cases double vision. The instructions indicate those who should not use them. The patches allow a slow release of the drug into the bloodstream, which minimizes side effects, but they are still there.

For that reason I prefer a combination of prescription drugs called Ephedrin and Promethezine. One is an "upper" and the other a "downer." They work so well against each other that I have no feeling that I've taken any drug—no drowsiness, no jag, no dry-mouth or any other effect except that it kills any feeling of seasickness. For me, they are very effective and unlike other drugs, I can wait until I feel sick before taking them. Again, these are available through prescription only. There are people—such as anyone with a heart condition—who should not take them. The problem with any drugs is that people have different reactions to them. I dislike taking drugs unless it's absolutely necessary.

Other anti-seasick tips include: 1) Stay in fresh air if there are alcohol, diesel or gas fumes below. 2) Sleep on your back rather than on your stomach. This seems to support the stomach better from bouncing around. 3) If you have a choice of berths, don't choose one in the forward cabin. There is less pitching motion in the center of the boat. The quietest berth is often the quarter-berth, if there is one. 4) Keep busy on deck rather than just sitting around thinking about it. 5) If you feel really terrible, tickle your throat over the lee side of the boat and get rid of it. Ask a crew member to hold on to your belt for support or use a safety harness. You'll be amazed at how much better you'll feel.

There are only a couple of other maladies that seem common on sailboats. One is constipation. It's usually only a problem on very long sails, because on others you get into port before the problem becomes acute. I've been on boats where a crew member hasn't gone in four or five days. For that reason a Fleet's enema is a good item to carry in the medical chest. It may be that unfamiliar sleeping habits caused by watch systems throws off other body functions in some people. Often the weather is so bad that using the head is a very uncomfortable process so you forego it for a day. That day is enough to plug most people up for the day after and so on. My only advice is to give it a try every day, particularly the first few days, no matter how uncomfortable the conditions.

The other common problem is sunburn on southern cruises. It's probably more of a problem on a boat than ashore because of the glare on the water. The cooling breeze makes you feel that the sun isn't as hot as it really is. Not much can be said that isn't obvious: cover up the first few days, use a sun lotion with a good sunscreen, and wear a hat. I have found the tennis-visor cap just great for this purpose. You can wear it low over the eyes, it doesn't come off easily and it is compact enough when folded to put in any pocket. If you wear sunglasses, be sure they're tied on and preferably not breakable.

It's a good idea to have a medical book aboard. Sailing is a great deal like mountaineering in that you have to be self sufficient often for long periods of time. There isn't a corner doctor's clinic you can run to if someone gets hurt. A good practical book with a lot of cross over to sailing is "Medicine for Mountaineering", the "bible" for travelers more than 24 hours away from medical aid. It's edited by Dr. James A. Wilkerson and obtainable through Offshore Sailing School, Ltd., Inc.

WEAK POINTS

Equipment breaks on a sailboat when the forces get great enough. One way of minimizing your chances of being hurt is anticipating what might break. One of the most common failures is of turning blocks. Often a spinnaker or genoa sheet leads aft through a block and then forward to a winch. If the shackle holding the block lets go or breaks, the rig becomes a big slingshot with the block as the missile. I know of a teenager aboard a cruising boat who was badly injured when a turning block was flung into his head. So don't stand forward of or in the bight of a turning block. Even if the sheet only pops out of the block, it can trip you up if you're standing in the bight and flip you overboard.

Another area of weakness is the main boom gooseneck. There is a tremendous strain there and in a heavy blow closehauled they have been known to rip off the boom and fly to leeward. I know of another man who was hurt when the gooseneck failed and the boom hit him in the head. Avoid, therefore, walking forward or aft along the leeward side of the boat in heavy winds.

UP THE MAST

Every year there are accidents involving people climbing or being hoisted up masts to retrieve a lost halyard or to check the rigging for damage. The agile sailor who climbs up the mast hand over hand and holds on to the top of the mast while accomplishing the task at hand often forgets that hands can and do cramp up and involuntarily lose their grip. The only safe way to go up is in a "Bosun's chair" and in rolling conditions even using a chair can be dangerous if not done properly. The chair is usually a piece of board to sit on with two lines from each end (like a child's swing) that dead-end in an eye a few feet up.

Attach the jib halyard to the eye in the Bosun's chair. A safety line should be spliced to the eye of the chair and tied to the eye in the halyard that holds the snap-shackle. Thus, if the shackle failed or opened, you'd still be attached. If the conditions are very bad, it's a good idea to tape the snap-shackle closed because the "pull" could easily catch on something as you go up and pull the pin thereby opening the shackle.

Your next problem is to be sure that if you lose your grip on the mast on the way up you won't be swinging around like a paddle-ball on the end of a rubber band. The mast describes a big arc in a rough sea and it's not only hard to hold on, but if you let go you can be swinging wildly out of control. It happened to a friend of mine who went up in a blow to cut free a wrapped spinnaker. He ended up spinning around an upper shroud all wrapped up in the halyard and unconscious. I use two methods to avoid this mishap. First, always have a downhaul line attached to the bottom of the chair with a crew member feeding out slack in the line as you go. Second, snap a snatch block to the eye of the chair where the halyard is attached. Snap the block over any other halyard that runs all the way up the mast so it doesn't have to be disconnected mid-way up. If no other halyard is available, then snap the block over the one that's taking you up. This isn't as desirable as there's no way of snubbing the halyard in tight since it's pulling you up.

As you go up remember that the halyard could part (break). There's an old axiom, "One hand for the boat and one for yourself," which means, "hold on!" Wherever possible accomplish the task with one hand so you can save yourself with the other if something gives.

CREW OVERBOARD

With extensive research and trials on the water, the U.S. Yacht Racing Union Safety-at-Sea Committee, the U.S. Naval Academy Sailing Squadron, the Cruising Club of America Technical Committee and the Sailing Foundation of Seattle, Washington joined forces to find the most effective way to save a person who has fallen overboard.

The result is two methods: the "quick-stop" and the "Seattle Sling" methods. With full crews the fastest is the "quick-stop", but with shorthanded crews or in extreme weather conditions the surest and safest is the Seattle sling.

QUICK-STOP METHOD:

1. Shout "man overboard" and, if available, designate a crew-member to spot the victim's position in the water. The spotter should not take his eyes off the victim (figure 59).
2. Provide immediate flotation. Deploy buoyed objects such as cockpit cushions, rolled up PFDs kept handy to the helmsman, life rings and so on. These objects may not only come to the aid of the victim, but will "litter the water" where the crew member went overboard and help your spotter to keep the crew member in view. It was determined that deployment of the standard man-overboard pole rig required too much time. The pole rig is saved to "put on top" of the victim in case the initial maneuver is unsuccessful.
3. IMMEDIATELY bring boat head-to-wind and beyond (figure 59) without touching or easing the jib sheet or mainsheet.
4. Allow the jib to back and further slow the boat.
5. Continue the turn with headsail backed until wind is abaft the beam.
6. Course is stabilized on this beam-to-broad reach for two or three lengths then altered to nearly dead downwind.
7. Drop the headsails while keeping the mainsail centered (or nearly so). The jib sheets are not slacked, even during the dousing maneuver, to keep them inside the lifelines.
8. Hold the downwind course until victim is abaft the beam.
9. Jibe the boat.
10. Approach the victim on a course of approximately 45 to 60 degrees off the wind.
11. Establish contact with the victim with a heaving line or other device. The Naval Academy uses a "throwing sock" containing 75 feet of light floating line and a kapok bag that can be thrown into the wind because the line is kept inside the bag and trails out as it sails to the victim.
12. Effect recovery over the leeward side.

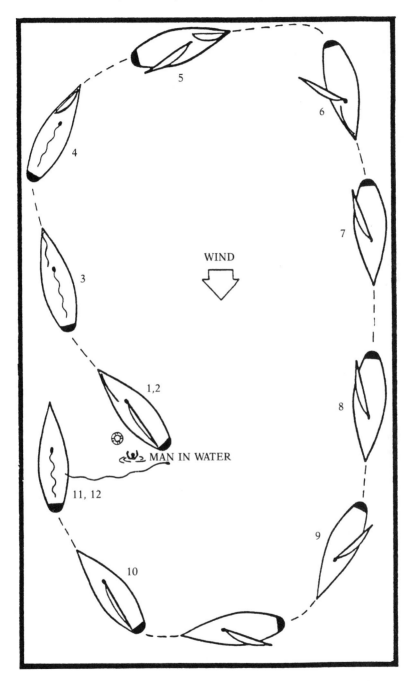

FIGURE 59

TWELVE STEPS TO A QUICK MAN-OVER-BOARD RECOVERY

–Spinnakers–

The same procedure is used to accommodate a boat sailing under spinnaker. Follow the preceding instructions. As the boat comes head-to-wind and the pole is eased quickly to the head stay, the spinnaker halyard is quickly lowered and the sail is gathered on the foredeck. The turn is continued through the tack and the approach phase commences.

–Yawls and Ketches–

Experiment with your mizzensail. During sea trials it was determined that the best procedure was to drop the mizzen as soon as it is convenient to do so during the early phases of Quick-Stop.

–Use of the Engine–

The use of the engine is not required although it is advisable to start the diesel but to keep it in neutral during the Quick-Stop phase unless it is needed in the final approach.

LIFE-SLING METHOD:

The life-sling is a specialized piece of equipment. It consists of a floating horsecollar device that doubles as a hoisting sling. The life sling is attached to the boat by a length of floating line three or four times the boat's length. When a crewmember falls overboard the scenario should proceed as follows:

1. A cushion or other flotation is thrown while the boat is brought IMMEDIATELY head-to-wind, slowed and stopped (figure 60).
2. The Seattle Sling is deployed by opening the bag that is hung on the stern pulpit and dropping the sling into the water. It will trail out astern and draw out the remaining line.
3. Once deployed, the boat is sailed in a wide circle around the victim with the line and sling trailing astern. The jib is not tended but allowed to back from the head-to-wind position, which increases the rate of turn.

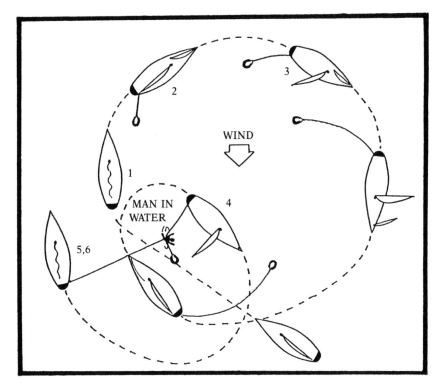

FIGURE 60

SIX STEPS TO A MAN-OVERBOARD RECOVERY FOR A SHORTHANDED CREW.

4. Contact is established with the victim by the line and sling being drawn inward by the boat's circling motion. The victim then places the sling over his head and under his arms.
5. Upon contact, the boat is put head-to-wind again, the headsail is dropped to the deck and the main is doused.
6. As the boat drifts slowly backward, the crew begins pulling the sling and the victim to the boat. If necessary, a cockpit winch can be used to assist in this phase, which should continue until the victim is alongside and pulled up tightly until suspended in the sling and cannot drop out. Then a block and tackle arrangement is attached to a halyard and the sling to lift the victim aboard.

Both these methods should be practiced, so your crew will automatically make the proper response if someone falls overboard. Otherwise the crew will be paralyzed by inaction when the incident happens.

GROUNDING

There are very few people who have sailed extensively who haven't been aground at one time or another. Most of the groundings are not dangerous. It only becomes dangerous if you fetch up on a lee shore with wind and sea pushing you further aground on a rocky bottom. If there's no sea or rocks, often it's just a matter of waiting for the tide to come in and lift you off. Many marinas are up narrow creeks with shifting bottoms and it's here that the most common grounding occurs. Another reason for running aground is not watching the chart carefully enough. Most new sailors assume that the further they are from shore the deeper the water is, so they don't even look at the chart when they get a good distance out. Get in the habit of always looking at the chart, particularly when you see a buoy. A buoy could mark a spot that's 30' deep in surrounding water 100' deep or it could mark a nearby rock or shoal that's only a couple of feet under the surface. Yet to most sailors it all looks like deep water well away from shore. In the Virgin Islands I know of a case where cruising sailors, out in a 20–25 knot breeze and having trouble, spotted a quiet harbor with boats anchored in it and headed right for it without looking at the chart. This is the height of foolishness and irresponsibility. Most such harbors are only good because they're being protected by a reef which has a narrow opening somewhere along it. Yet the water looks the same as deep water (if you're heading into the sun) so you must watch the chart carefully. The boat I was talking about above, a 35 footer, ran right up on the reef and pounded for several hours before it could be towed off. Thousands of dollars of damage was done.

If you run aground and the tide is going out, the first few minutes are the crucial ones. An auxiliary sailboat has little power in reverse so you're probably wasting precious time trying to back off. Put the helm hard over so the boat will turn towards deep water and rev up the engine in forward gear. If the sails are up, trim them in tight to heel the boat to raise its draft. Adjust the sails to help rotate the boat. Rock the boat by having the crew lean way out over one side hanging onto shrouds. If this doesn't work, quickly take the anchor out in the dinghy and drop it in deep water. Then pull the boat off by using the powerful jib sheet winches. Surprisingly enough, using the dinghy tugboat-style is very effective. That is, push the sailboat sideways with the bow of the dinghy against the side of the sailboat near its bow.

If none of the above works the boat has to be heeled more. Carry the anchor out in the dinghy straight abeam and drop it.

Tie a loop in the middle of the line and attach a halyard. Winch on the halyard and this should pull the mast over, heeling the boat and possibly breaking it free. Do not do this with a main halyard from a fractional rig as the mast does not have enough support.

If all the above fails and no other boat is around to pull you off you may have to settle down and wait for the tide to come in again. If you went aground near high tide, you'll have to wait close to twelve hours on the U.S. east coast. Also you'll be almost high and dry at low tide. The danger is that, as the tide comes in, water will fill up the boat. All hatches and hatchboards have to be closed so no water can get in.

STEERING PROBLEMS

It's fairly common to have the steering fail on a boat, particularly one with a wheel. You should inspect it often to see if there are any bad portions of wire on the steering quadrant. Be careful not to store anything in the quadrant area that could fall or jam into the steering when the boat heels. Sometimes it falls next to the quadrant and you don't realize it until you're in a docking maneuver and need full rudder. Then you find you can only turn the rudder $2/3$ of the way. Obviously, this can be not only embarrassing, but dangerous.

If the steering fails and you're in relatively shallow water, head into the wind and anchor immediately. Then, at your leisure, you can make repairs. In deep water you'll have to steer by the sails for a while until you either fix the steering or insert the emergency tiller. The latter is usually inserted onto the top of the rudder post through a plate-covered opening near the steering pedestal. Be sure you have practiced using the emergency tiller so no time is lost. Seconds could be precious in many cases.

The repair might be impossible to make as in the case of a lost rudder. Then it's necessary to steer by the sails as described in Offshore Sailing School's basic manual, *"Colgate's Basic Sailing."* On a cruising boat the theory is the same. Ease the main and trim the jib to bring the center of effort (C.E.) forward and fall off. Trim the main and ease the jib to bring the C.E. aft to head up or to tack. If you want to sail off the wind and your charterboat has a forestaysail, trim it amidships. It will help directional control by keeping your bow heading downwind. If the boat starts to come up, the staysail will fill and push the bow down. When the boat starts to jibe, the staysail will push the bow back before the main comes across. The trim of the staysail has to be varied slightly depending upon the downwind course desired. A jib can be used instead of a staysail.

A steering emergency occurred one year during a flotilla charter of our Offshore Sailing School graduates in Greece. The cruise was being led by our then Operations Director, Rob Eberle. He noticed that one of the boats appeared to be in trouble and was sailing toward shallow water off a point of land. He immediately raised her on the radio and asked the problem. The girl who responded was a fairly recent grad and she said they had lost their steering. Rob asked if she remembered from the "Learn to Sail" course how to tack a boat without using the rudder. She said, "Yes, luff the jib and trim the main," to which Rob replied, "Do it! Now!" He was delighted to see the boat tack and sail away from the shallow water. The point is, since it is possible to steer with the sails it is not a disaster to lose your steering. Every skipper should practice sailing without touching the steering wheel or tiller so that should a failure occur, he or she will know just how the boat handles when steered by the sails alone and would be able to guide her into safe water or to port. Unless you practice, it's easy to panic and end up in trouble. Most important about steering failure is don't panic. Boats have sailed thousands of miles without rudders, so figure you can too.

RIGHT OF WAY

The first defense against collisions is proper vigilance. There are blind spots on sailboats to leeward behind the sails so the skipper must assign a crew as a lookout in areas where he or she can't see. The second defense is knowledge of the right of way rules—second because such knowledge is of no help if you hit a boat you failed to see.

It's very easy to be lulled into complacency on the water. Everything is so peaceful and quiet. But if you are sailing at six knots and another boat way off, two miles away, hardly more than a speck, is approaching you at six knots, in ten minutes you both could collide. So every few minutes, sweep the horizon for other boats.

As for the rules, let's start with power. A cruising sailboat under power is classified as a motorboat and is liable to the motorboat "rules of the road" as the right of way rules are called. Even if you have your sails up and are "motor-sailing" as long as the engine is in gear the motorboat rules apply.

Though there are many minor ramifications, the main thing to remember when motorboats are on a converging collision course is that the one in the other's "danger zone" has the right of way. The "danger zone" of a motorboat is from dead ahead to two points abaft the starboard beam (figure 61). If there is any boat approaching from that area you must avoid it. It is the "stand-on" vessel in that it has the right of way, and you are the "give-way" vessel in that you must keep clear. The obligation of the "stand-on" vessel is to hold its course and speed so they won't be misled in the other's attempt to keep clear.

The other most common motorboat rule to remember is that if two vessels are approaching almost head-on, each will avoid the other by turning to starboard. It's most important to make your

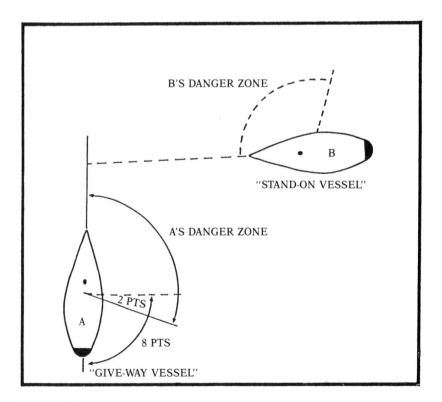

FIGURE 61

BOAT B IS IN A'S DANGER ZONE (FROM DEAD AHEAD TO TWO POINTS ABAFT THE STARBOARD BEAM) AND THEREFORE HAS RIGHT OF WAY.

intentions very clear to the other skipper. A sharp turn to starboard followed by a gradual turn back to your original course will indicate to him that you plan to pass port to port (your port side passing his port side.) Motorboats use horn signals for passing and, legally, sailboats under power should too. As a practical matter, though, the horn is usually buried in a bucket or tool kit somewhere and not handy. Therefore, make sure your turns clearly indicate your course intentions. One other common motorboat rule is the overtaking rule. A boat catching up to another from any point aft of the danger zone is overtaking and must keep clear of the overtaken boat.

The rule covering sail versus power is quite simple. Almost every sailor knows that a sailboat has right-of-way over a motorboat. However, not many seem to know that there are a number of exceptions to this rule. If the motorboat is anchored, is disabled, or is being overtaken by a sailboat, the motorboat is the privileged vessel. A commercial vessel with limited maneuverability in a narrow channel and a commercial fishing boat trawling also have right-of-way over a sailboat.

A slightly more complicated set of rules governs two sailboats meeting one another. There are three basic possibilities covered by three rules: (1) if sailboats are converging on the same tack, the leeward boat has right-of-way; (2) if they are converging on opposite tacks, the starboard tack boat has right-of-way; and (3) as in motorboats, the overtaken boat (the boat ahead) has right-of-way over the overtaking boat.

So how do we know if we're on a collision course? Take a bearing on the other boat either by using your compass or by lining it up with a shroud, stanchion, or other fixed item on your boat. If, a little while later, the bearing hasn't changed and you haven't altered your course or speed, then you are on a collision course. That the boats are traveling at different speeds makes no difference. Boat A in figure 62 is obviously sailing faster than Boat B but the compass bearing of 070 degrees hasn't changed, so they are destined to collide. If A takes a second bearing and it's 080 degrees and then 090 degrees, A will cross ahead of B. If the numbers decrease, then B will cross A.

Another way of judging whether you are on a collision course is to sight land in the distance behind the other boat. If land is disappearing behind the bow of the boat, she will cross you. If land is appearing in front of the bow (as if she was going backwards against the backdrop of the land), you will cross her. If the land remains stationary, watch out! You are on a collision course.

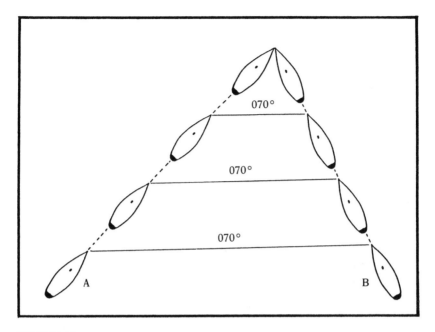

FIGURE 62

COLLISION COURSE WHEN THE BEARING DOESN'T CHANGE—SPEED MAKES NO DIFFERENCE.

NIGHT SAILING

Almost all charter companies insist that there be no sailing at night aboard their boats. Their insurance does not cover it. However, on the assumption that persons taking our courses may sail at night in their own or friend's boats, we will briefly review it here.

For those used to city and suburban electrical illumination at night, the thought of sailing at night at sea is that of sailing in pitch black darkness. Such is not the case. Even with total cloud cover, visibility is rather good and on some moonlit nights one can see perfectly for miles, much like being in daylight wearing dark sunglasses.

In certain parts of the country, Long Island Sound, for instance, there are so many navigation lights that it's virtually impossible to get lost at night. Just be sure to follow the charts carefully and steer an accurate compass course. Count the number of seconds between flashes of the light you've spotted. Let's say you've seen a light flash. Count "One thousand and one, one thousand and two, one thousand and three," etc. until it flashes again. This should give you the number of seconds between flashes. You could use a stopwatch, but then you'd have to use a flashlight or go below to read it. Either way your night vision is impaired momentarily for further sightings. The navigator should never give the crew on deck the characteristics of the light he wishes to find. If he says he's looking for a four-second white flashing light just off the starboard bow, the person spotting is apt to accept that the light he sees is the one the navigator wants him to see. However, if he sees a light off the starboard bow and the navigator insists that the spotter determine the characteristics himself there is much less chance for error.

One major danger in night sailing is collisions. It's imperative that anyone who sails at night knows and can read navigation lights. The basic lights that most all vessels have are red and green sidelights. These are "ten point" lights and can be seen from dead ahead to two points abaft the beam. There are 32 points in the compass (11 1/4 degrees each) and 8 points to a quadrant. The red is on the port side (often remembered by the fact that port wine is red) and the green on starboard. A sailboat will carry only sidelights and a white stern light. Under power she has to carry a steaming light. Larger powerboats carry a steaming light and also a higher range light. The relationship between these two lights tell the observer which way the boat is turning.

Some special lights are very important to know. For instance, if you see three vertical lights in a row you can be sure it's a tug with a tow. The tow should have side lights and a sternlight, but they are often very weak and hard to see. Be sure you know where the tow is. If you pass behind the tug you may hit the tow line, or, worse yet, you may be smashed by the barge.

When you see two vertical lights, the barge is either alongside the tug, or less than 200 meters astern. This situation poses much less of a threat since you can quite easily spot the last barge in the line. The lights mentioned here are only a few of the possibilities. Study the U.S. Coast Guard Navigation Rules for the rest.

A green light above a white light indicates a trawler dragging his nets, for instance. When dragging, this boat has right-of-way over all the others, including sailboats, so be careful to avoid him.

Reading lights (determining the course, speed and type of boat from his lights) takes experience. If you don't have it you shouldn't venture out at night without someone on board with such experience. Someone has to determine if you're on a collision course and if you have right-of-way in order to make the proper decision as to course change. A wrong decision could be disastrous, so don't take sailing at night lightly. When it looks like there may be a close call developing, and the other vessel may not be aware of your existence, play your spotlight over your sails for several minutes so the other vessel's skipper can see them. This works well in good visibility, but it's next to useless in bad weather (when you most need to be seen). It is more effective to shine the spotlight right at the wheelhouse of the other vessel. From this vantage point, the battery-operated spotlight will look like a pinprick of light, if it is seen at all. It certainly won't blind the helmsman—which you obviously want to avoid—but it will make him aware that there is a boat out there.

Your binoculars, which you use so frequently during daylight, can also be very useful at dusk or at night. I was in a situation not too long ago where we were converging with a number of commercial boats and it was hard to tell exactly what they were doing. The lights seemed close together and confusing, and no wonder. By checking with binoculars we found that we could cross one tug towing a barge and then safely sail between it and another tug towing a barge to windward of the first tug and tow. The binoculars made the situation very clear.

It's not common knowledge how one properly focuses binoculars, so a synopsis might be appropriate here. First cover the right lens and adjust the focus for your left eye with the center focus adjustment. Then cover the left lens and adjust the focus for your right eye with the focusing ring on the right eyepiece. Now you're ready to focus for both eyes with the center focus adjustment.

In another situation, we were converging at dusk with a ship that was lit up like a Christmas tree. We could not pick up the side lights and had no idea which way she was going. A check with the binoculars showed the boat to be a large sailing schooner (with a generator, which accounted for all the lights), and we easily set a course to avoid her. When you have the experience and feel at ease, some of the most beautiful, peaceful sailing is at night—a really rewarding experience.

Chapter 6

CRUISING

In effect, everything we've told you so far will help you cruise. However, there are a few specific hints that may help you out.

WATER

Modern charter boats have hundreds of gallons of water, so water conservation isn't as necessary as it used to be. There may be as many as five water tanks with valve handles to turn when one runs out and another is needed. Use them one at a time starting with the one furthest forward. Pitching will be reduced when sailing if the forward water tank is empty. If they are all turned on at once and some hose develops a leak you could lose *all* your water into the bilge instead of losing just one tank. A tank is almost empty when the pressure pump runs continually after you have turned off a faucet. It should run only a short time to build up pressure and then turn itself off automatically. Turn on the valve to a full tank and turn on a spigot. The pressure pump will run and water will spurt out combined with air until all the air is bled out. You may have to open a number of spigots to get all the air out of the system and close them off one by one when you get a steady flow of water. Then turn off the last open spigot. The pump will run until adequate pressure is restored and then turn itself off.

Using some water conservation efforts will avoid the need to refill the tanks during the charter. For instance, don't run the water in the shower for long periods. Just wet yourself down, lather up with the shower off and then rinse the soap off.

Better yet, swim off the stern washing with a liquid detergent like Joy, which lathers well in saltwater, and rinse off with the deck shower. The deck shower usually has a handle you hold down to use. When you put it away in it's cubbyhole, make sure you don't jam the handle so it runs. If you do, you'll probably hear the water pump running and figure out the problem. If you stowed the shower and immediately went ashore, you wouldn't hear it and could lose all your water—at least in one tank.

Wash dishes by stopping the sink. There are usually two sinks side by side. Have soapy water and wash in one side. Rinse with clean water in the other. If you're really low on water, take a bucket and wash the dishes in salt water, assuming you're in clean water. Then rinse with fresh water.

If you want to wash your hair, do it while swimming off the stern. It uses far less water and works well. I recommend rinsing off with the fresh water deck shower, because salt water becomes a bit itchy after it dries on your skin.

It's a good idea to turn the water pump electrical switch off at night. If someone gets water in the middle of the night, the racket of the water pump can wake everybody else up. Most charter-boats have a manual or foot operated backup pump that is very quiet to use and should be used at night.

I also suggest topping off the water tanks before you leave on the charter, just to be sure the dock staff filled all your tanks.

And turn off the water pump switch when leaving the boat for long periods of time. If a leak developed while you were gone and one of the tanks emptied into the bilge, the water pump would run continuously trying vainly to build up pressure and would burn out.

COOKING AND THE GALLEY

BARBECUE GRILL

In charter areas where there are not many restaurants, you will be cooking aboard for a number of meals. Most charters use a barbecue grill that hangs over the stern for a lot of the cooking: hamburgers, chicken, steak, fish, etc. To keep the grill clean for the next use, line the bottom with aluminum foil. Put the charcoal (usually the self-starting egg carton type) on top and light. The heat put out is not excessive, so it's a good idea to boil chicken on the stove below before barbecuing. Otherwise, the charcoal embers may die before the chicken is cooked through, particularly in a windy area. Remember that the grill must only be used at anchor. The boat lines up with the wind causing smoke and sparks to drift harmlessly astern away from the boat. Never use the grill at a dock even if the wind direction is initially safe. A windshift could blow sparks over the boat or on to adjacent boats. Your grill will usually be at one corner of the stern. Hang your dinghy from the opposite corner or along the other side, so ashes and sparks don't fall into it.

STOVES

The most common stoves on sailboats being used for charter are fueled by CNG (compressed natural gas) or LPG (liquid petroleum gas, currently known as propane). Most charter companies in the U.S. and Caribbean use CNG. This is the safest and most efficient fuel. It is safer than propane because it is lighter than air. If there's a leak in the system, CNG will dissipate rather than drop to the lowest part of the bilge, as propane, where any spark such as from the engine starter motor or an open flame can cause an explosion. Alcohol stoves are fairly safe, because an achohol fire can be extinguished by water, but they are inefficient with a cool flame compared to gas. Most gas stoves use a solenoid switch that turns the fuel off at the tank on deck. It's best to turn the solenoid off when you're finished cooking before you turn the burners off. This burns the fuel out of the line and, when the flames go out, you know that the solenoid switch has worked properly. Then turn off the burners. European boats use propane, so if you smell gas, be sure not to make a spark.

Usually there are two fuel tanks. When one runs out, you unscrew the gas line from one tank and screw it on the full tank. The threads are *backwards* from your normal threads (left is tight and right is loose). NEVER do this operation when the barbecue is being used. One charter boat was lost that way.

REFRIGERATION

Modern charter sailboats have good refrigeration and the checkout person will tell you how long to charge the batteries or, if it's a mechanical cooling unit, how long to run the engine to keep it cold. When storing provisions, thought should be given to the order in which they will be used and then stored in reverse order. Cooling temperatures are quickly lost when excessive time is needed to find an item deeply buried. Replace cold drinks as they are used, so you don't have to add many warm ones when you run out.

Avoid the buildup of frost on the freezing compartment plates. A heavy layer of frost will act as insulation between the freezing and cooling compartments reducing the effectiveness of the latter. If frost builds up, run the refrigerator for less time or fewer times a day.

Leave all cardboard boxes ashore because roaches like to hide in them. Once roaches get on your boat they're hard to get rid of.

Use an ice bucket at cocktail time, so you aren't constantly opening the refrigerator to get ice for individual drink refills.

HEAD OPERATION

One simple rule to make on a cruising boat is that the head door will be hooked open unless in use. This has two results: 1) It allows fresh air to circulate through the head and 2) one knows just by looking below whether the head is in use or not.

Another rule to impress on the crew is that only two things are ever flushed: 1) Toilet paper and 2) that which has already been eaten. Anything else can clog it up, including paper towels and sanitary napkins. He who clogs it, cleans it! You only need to go through the messy job of taking a head apart once and you'll be a believer for life. Besides, if you don't unclog it a charter company usually charges a fee to fix the problem. Before using, pull the lever upright and pump clean water into the bowl. Make sure the thru-hull valves are open. If there is a high loop in the line, they may be left open when sailing. If not, they should be closed until use. After using, pump until the bowl is flushed clean. After it's clean, keep on pumping the handle for at least 10 to 15 strokes. This flushes any sewage right through the system and out the hull or into the holding tank.

Now push the valve lever forward and pump the bowl dry, so the water won't spill over the lip of the bowl as the boat heels. If there is any urine splatter or fecal residue on the bowl, it should be cleaned up right away with toilet paper and reflushed. A boat's head is small and has very poor ventilation. Any uncleaned residue around the bowl or in the system will soon start to smell very badly. Plus, it's a courtesy to the next person who uses it that he receives it clean and leaves it clean.

Keep a box of safety matches in the head and strike one or two after you're finished. They are an excellent deodorant. Be sure to pour some water on the dead match before tossing in the waste basket. Never try to flush it down the toilet.

You're sailing in beautiful tropical waters and have anchored in a quiet cove for lunch in the heat of the noon day sun. Two things happen: most of the crew dive off the stern for a refreshing swim and one crew member, who has been holding it all morning goes below for their "morning constitution". Needless to say the crew in the water are slightly upset to find "pollution" drifting in their midst. The obvious rule is "don't use the head when friends are swimming". It sounds so obvious, why should I waste space writing about it? Because people invariably forget or tend to equate the boat's head with their home toilet which carries waste away.

OTHER WASTE

There was a time when sailors dumped all their garbage overboard and thought nothing of it. Of course, that was before plastics and most that went over the side was biodegradable. With plastic, times have changed. Plastic can float around for centuries before decomposing.

Thus in December, 1988 the first international agreement to clean up the oceans went into effect when the U.S. ratified it by passing Public Law 100–200. Under the agreement called the MARPOL (for marine pollution) Protocol, Annex V it is illegal for any vessel to dump plastic anywhere in the ocean. Violators can be fined up to $50,000. It is illegal to dump garbage (victual waste), paper, rags, glass, metal, bottles, crockery and similar refuse inside of 12 miles from the nearest land.

Most charter companies and countries where chartering is common adhere strongly to the Protocol. After all, it's in their best interests and that of the charterers that the waters stay pristine, so future charterers can also enjoy the same beauty of those before. You should be provided with sufficient garbage bags. Use them. When they fill up, put them in an empty lazarette locker or, if it's very smelly, tow it astern in the dinghy. Then take the bags ashore to locations that accept them.

Even the BOC sailors, sailing singlehanded around the world have a pact not to toss any plastic over the side. The bandwagon is rolling. Let's keep it going.

As for discharge of sewage, it's more difficult to control. Boats are supposed to have an MSD (marine sanitation devise) in the U.S. as of 1980, but not all do. Compliance is poor because the law is perceived as poorly conceived. Eventually the bugs will be worked out and good MSDs invented. The EPA and Coast Guard studies indicate there is insufficient quantitative evidence that discharge from vessels under 65 feet in length constitute a national environmental problem. Therefore, the problem is being dealt with on a regional or local level. Just adhere with whatever the charter company says to do during your charter, because they will be up on the local laws and customs.

SAFETY BELOWDECKS

For fire protection, all charterboats have several well-placed extinguishers—i.e., not stowed next to the stove or engine that might catch fire, but yet within easy reach to be grabbed quickly. Learn their location before you depart. Also, every boat should have two easy means of egress from belowdecks in case one is blocked by the fire. On one of our flotilla cruises in the B.V.I., our boat suddenly developed a starter-motor fire. I pulled away the companionway steps and was on my knees spraying away with the fire extinguisher when I felt a lady's foot in the small of my back. With one bound she was out in the cockpit. We had a good chuckle about my qualities as a ladder. However, had she thought of it, she could have exited through the forward hatch.

A more frequent below deck hazard than fire is scalding. A friend of mine was boiling water while underway in a sailboat and had not thought that conditions warranted releasing the pins to allow the stove to gimbal. A powerboat wake caused the pot of boiling water to spill on his bare arm. He now has deep burn scars that look as though they had been caused by fire. To avoid such a problem, always let the stove gimbal when in use and secure the pots with the provided clamps. Some people wear foul weather gear during galley duty underway, but it's hot and I feel that's like wearing a helmet in your car on the highway in case you have an accident. The inconvenience outweighs the chance something will happen.

There's a greater possibility of scalding when pouring or spooning hot liquid from one receptacle to another. Do as air stewardesses do—never pour into a cup someone else is holding. The same person should always hold both pot and cup, so the pouring and holding hands move in concert. That way the left hand literally knows what the right is doing.

Slipping is another belowdecks hazard and it usually occurs when the cabin sole is wet. Thus, it's a good idea to make a rule that all wet clothing, boots and gear be removed and stowed in one assigned area rather than allowed to drip throughout the cabin. Also, if the sole does get wet, it should be wiped dry as soon as possible. Bare feet also add to your chances of slipping; deck shoes should be the rule at all times. Many people are injured by falls when the boat lurches during a knockdown or broach, but the boatwise crew will always know just where the ceiling handrail is, particularly in the area of the companionway.

SWIMMING AND FISHING

Most bareboat charter cruising boats are well designed for swimming with ladders off the stern, stern lazarettes for snorkels and fins and rinse-off showers nearby. In the Caribbean, it's a good idea to swim and check the anchor, a good excuse to get cool. Be careful about swimming where there are many outboard runabouts. I almost got run down swimming in Turkey off the bow of sailboats anchored stern-to the land. A large Zodiac with a 50 hp outboard came out from between two boats at full bore and never saw me. Unfortunately they only have two speeds in most parts of the world—stop and full speed ahead. Two days later from a restaurant on Marmaris Harbor we saw a swimming Turk get run down by a similar craft and badly hurt.

I've been advised, and I'm passing it on, not to wear shiny, glittery items such as watches or jewelry in the water because they attract barracuda. This may or may not be true. I always wear a watch, have seen barracuda and have not been bothered and I know of a woman who was sleeping on a beach with her feet extending out in the water (no jewelry) who was attacked. Maybe they just know who's tastier.

Here's a tip if you're swimming in to a beach bar or restaurant and need to take money. The little cannisters that hold 35 mm slide film are completely watertight. Fold up some currency, put it in an empty cannister, tuck it in your bathing suit and swim ashore.

When you get near the beach or shore, watch out for sea urchins, the black spiny balls in the rocks. The spines penetrate the skin and break off like splinters. Meat tenderizer is the cure. Pour it liberally on the puncture. If you don't have meat tenderizer, lime juice works well.

Shell collectors on charter in the Pacific or Indian Oceans must be careful with cone shaped shells with a textile color pattern (rather than solid) and a bright red proboscis. If you pick them up, avoid the open end, the head. Wear gloves since the proboscis of some species can reach the back of the shell. At least four species are known to have caused death by heart failure.

Found in the Caribbean is ciquatoxic fish poisoning. Ciquatera only occurs in tropical marine reef fish, especially those with a parrotlike beak. In order of incidence, it occurs most in the following fish: barracuda, snapper, jack and grouper (7%). You shouldn't have trouble eating fish in a restaurant, but don't eat any reef fish you've caught or speared yourself. If the fish tastes bad, don't eat it. The symptoms are very unpleasant, including convulsions. Death occurs in 7% of the cases reported.

There is some truth to the old adage of avoiding shell fish in the months that do not have an "r" in them . . . that is, in temperate oceans in the Northern Hemisphere. When there's a "red tide" bloom and a lot of dead fish floating on the surface or washed on the beaches, shellfish can be affected for months after the "red tide" has disappeared. It's called paralytic shellfish poisoning and death has occurred in 10–25% of the cases reported.

Jellyfish are usually fairly harmless, but I have received stings that make it look like I was lashed by a cat-o-nine tails. The welts sting, but it subsides quickly. Avoid going near the Man O'War jellyfish that have the pretty semi-circular "sail" on the surface of the water and tentacles hanging down. Use vinegar or lime juice to neutralize a jellyfish sting.

Sting rays and skates are not aggressive, but many species have a barbed spine that's painful if stepped on. If you can't see the bottom, wear foot protection and shuffle rather than walk.

If you do get a venomous sting from fish or mollusks, clean and flush the puncture wound immediately. Urine, which is surprisingly sterile, can be used if there's no clean water. Urine is also effective on fire coral wounds we were told on a cruise of French Polynesia.

BERTHS

There are a few tricks to bedding down for a comfortable night on a boat at anchor. Many berths are covered by vinyl plastic or Naugahyde. Sheets slip on such surfaces and never seem to stay in place. You end up directly in contact with the plastic which has a cold and clammy feel. Others are covered with Herculon fabric which is tough but scratchy. First lay a blanket as a liner over the foam mattress. It isolates your bottom sheet from the mattress. Then make the bed as usual. If you are using regular twin-bed sized sheets and blankets, you can double them so that half is under and half is on top of you. Since you have a limited number of clean sheets on a cruise, this allow you to use them up half as fast.

If you go below for a snooze while sailing, be sure to tie up the lee canvases which form a restraining wall to keep you from falling out of the bunk. Remember, it's fine to sack out on the lee-ward side and not worry about the lee canvases, but that side can suddenly become the windward side due to a sudden windshift in a squall or because of a tack. Many charter boats don't have lee canvases, because charterers are not allowed to sail at night. In that case, select a quarter berth aft or the V-berth up forward where there's a vertical surface on either side and one can't fall out.

RADIOTELEPHONE

Every charterboat will have a marine radiotelephone aboard, usually very high frequency, VHF for short. The "call letters", like a serial number assigned to the radio by the government, should be posted next to the radio. Whenever you use the VHF, you should identify yourself with the boat name and then the call letters. If they're "WGH1756," you should say "Yacht Alfa, Yacht Alfa, Yacht Alfa, this is Yacht Bravo, whiskey-golf-hotel-one-seven-five-six. Over." Learn the phonetic alphabet (Appendix A). It's fun and easy. Always listen first before transmitting so you don't interrupt an emergency conversation.

The contact channel is channel 16 and once your party has responded, immediately arrange a mutually acceptable channel to switch to for conversation. Ship to ship channels are: 09, 12, 13, 14, 20, 65, 66, 68 and 73.

Do not talk on channel 16, because it is also the emergency channel. Your conversation could keep a "Mayday" from being heard and cause loss of life. This is happening with a frightening frequency recently. People either don't know courtesy or don't give a damn with the result that channel 16 is being clogged by extraneous chatter overwhelming the true emergency calls. Also, remember that calling "Mayday" means you have a life-threatening situation aboard. You *do not* call "Mayday" because you've run out of gas, but are otherwise safe. There are other levels of safety messages. "Mayday" is a distress call and has top priority. If you hear someone calling "Pan. Pan. Pan." it's an urgent message relating to the safety of a ship or person. The third level relates to safety of navigation or important weather warnings and the call is "Securite. Securite. Securite."

To set up your radio for calling or receiving, turn the on-off volume switch up high. Then turn the "squelch" knob up (clockwise) until you hear an awful blast of static noise. Then turn it down just enough to quiet the static. Often the inability to communicate with another radiotelephone is caused by the squelch knob being turned down too far, so make sure it's as high as possible without static noise.

Remember that your conversations can be heard by all other boats, so don't say anything embarrassing. Years ago we were anchored in a Connecticut harbor when a sailboat arrived crewed by a guy and an incredibly beautiful girl in a bikini. They anchored ahead of us. We were having cocktails, watching a beautiful sunset, with our radio on and we hear the yacht ahead of us call the marine operator and contact a private home. The conversation went something like this, "Honey, I can't get home tonight. I'm totally fogged in. I'll get back as soon as possible tomorrow". Privacy does not exist on the VHF, so be careful. It's also a federal offense to use profane language on the VHF.

When your conversation is finished say "This is Yacht Bravo, whiskey-golf-hotel-one-seven-five-six. Out" or "Standing by on channel 16."

Chapter 7

NAVIGATION

Navigation is broken down into two categories—celestial navigation and piloting. The former is navigation based on the position of the celestial bodies and is normally used out of sight of land. For navigation on bareboat cruises, we use piloting which is navigation by reference to landmarks, buoys, sounding and the like.

PILOTING

Coastwise navigation or "piloting" consists of transferring your actual position to an easily readable picture in the form of a chart. Basically it requires that you determine your position (called a "fix"), locate the fix on the chart and then use the rest of the chart to answer certain questions. The fix has answered the question "Where am I?", but an even more appropriate late question would be "Am I in safe water?". In other words, is there enough depth of water for the boat's draft, where are the nearest dangers to the boat such as rocks, reefs, shoals and riptides. From the chart you want to be able to determine a course or courses to steer that will allow a safe passage to deep water or to some other destination.

THE CHART

The chart is a neat "road map" of the sea printed by the U.S. Department of Commerce and available at many nautical supply stores. The area a chart covers and the identifying number is listed in the nautical chart catalog. Figure 63 shows a section of this catalog. If sailing the western end of Long Island Sound, for

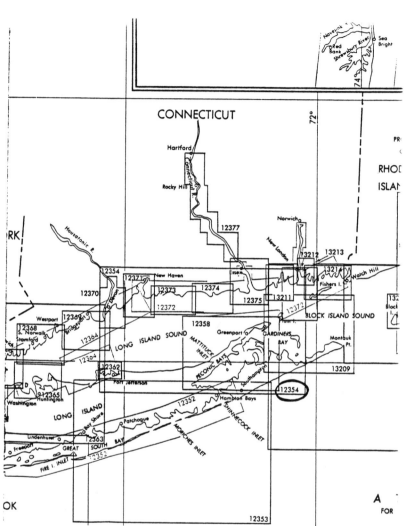

FIGURE 63

NAUTICAL CHART CATALOG

instance, look at the catalog sheet and note that chart #12354 is
needed (the circled number in figure 63).

For very small boats, the Small Craft Series of charts is handy
because they are prefolded compactly and don't need a large, flat
surface to spread on. Also, one chart covers the same area that a
number of the other charts cover, so they are more economical to
purchase. The only problem with the Small Craft Series of charts

is they don't give you the "big picture" of the area and it's often difficult to find the next adjoining chart when you run off the edge of the first. The less distinct outline with numbers such as "12372" in figure 63 show the coverage of Small Craft charts.

As can be seen in the catalog, charts come in different scales. They are all roughly the same physical size, but cover different sized areas. Chart #12375, for instance, covers only a small portion of chart #12354, yet blows it up to about the same size as #12354. Since #12375 enlarges a small area, it is called a "large scale" chart. Such charts are used for entering harbors where precision and accuracy is more necessary than when in open water. If you're planning a trip, a smaller scale chart covers more distance and is easier to use.

Though charts have many different scales, the most common are 1:80,000, 1:40,000, and 1:20,000. This means one foot on a 1 to 80,000 chart is equivalent to 80,000 feet on land or roughly 13 nautical miles.

On a 1 to 20,000 chart, one foot equals 20,000 feet or about 3.3 NM. Obviously there will be less detail when you crowd 13 miles into a foot of chart space than with 3.3 miles, so the latter is a large scale chart which shows more detail. The smaller the numbers, the larger the scale and vice versa.

The traditional equipment used are still parallel rulers and dividers. The former moves a course or bearing on the chart from the compass rose to your position or that of a landmark you sighted. Dividers measure distance. Though those two items and a pencil are all one needs, others have been developed that some sailors find helpful to use. If you cruise on a charterboat in Europe, you are not apt to find parallel rulers as part of the boat's navigation equipment. Instead there will be some form of protractor, a clear plastic rectangle with a compass rose in the middle. Lay one edge on the desired course and slide the center of the protracter over a meridian of longitude. The reading on the compass rose will be your true course as in figure 64. In this case the course between the bell and whistle buoy is 071 degrees or 251 degrees depending on which direction you are sailing. Remember to correct for variation.

DISTANCES

For the purpose of navigation the earth is considered to be a perfect sphere which is 21,600 nautical miles in circumference.

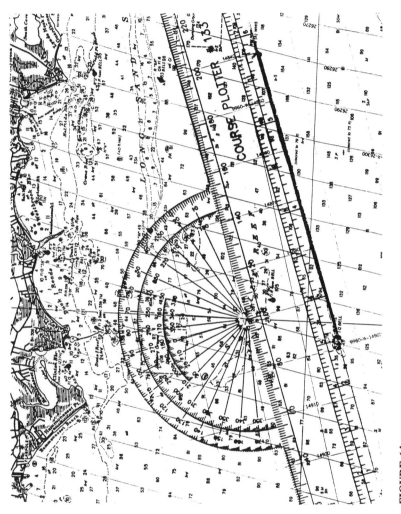

FIGURE 64

USING A PROTRACTOR TO ESTABLISH A TRUE COURSE.

The north pole is named for the top of the globe and the south pole is the bottom. Lines running north and south around the earth passing through these two imaginary poles are called meridians of longitude. The horizontal lines are parallels of latitude. Since a circle is 360 degrees, the parallel lines of latitude divide the earth into 360 equal parts of 60 nautical miles each. There are 60 minutes to a degree, so one minute of latitude is equivalent to one nautical mile, which is somewhat longer than the statute mile we use ashore. A statute mile is 5280 feet and a nautical mile is 6076 feet. To convert statute to nautical miles, multiply by 0.87. For example, 50 statute miles is 43.5 nautical miles (50 x 0.87). To convert nautical to statute miles, multiply by 1.2. In other words, 50 nautical miles is 60 statute miles (50 x 1.2). This is the same when converting knots to miles per hour and vice versa. If you are sailing 10 knots, that's 12 MPH (10 x 1.2). If you are in a speedboat going 44 MPH, you are traveling 38 knots (44 x 0.87). These numbers have been rounded off for ease of use. The latter example would be 38.2357 knots if accuracy were important, but we rarely deal with such pinpoint accuracy in marine navigation.

To measure the distance between points A and B in figure 65 we use a pair of dividers. We place one tip on point A and the other on point B. Now place the dividers along the edge of the chart and count the number of minutes of latitude (shown as alternate dark and light increments, each divided into tenths) that fall between two tips. In this case it's 3.6 minutes. If we sail that distance in one half hour, we are sailing at 7.2 knots. A knot is one nautical mile sailed in one hour.

If the distance you want to measure is greater than the spread attainable by the dividers, spread them along the edge of the chart a workable number of miles (minutes of latitude), say five miles from tip to tip. Then lay one tip on your starting point. The other will rest on a spot five miles down the course. "Walk" the dividers down the course until your destination is reached. It would be unusual for the last measurement to be exactly five miles, so the dividers will probably have to be pressed together so the tip rests on the destination. This reduced distance is measured on the edge of the chart.

To measure long distances on a 1:80,000 scale chart where only a rough estimation of distance is needed, I use my hand. The spread between my thumb and little finger is almost exactly 10 miles and I can measure 70 to 80 mile distances quickly and within a few miles of accuracy. Check your hand spread. Perhaps you can use this method also.

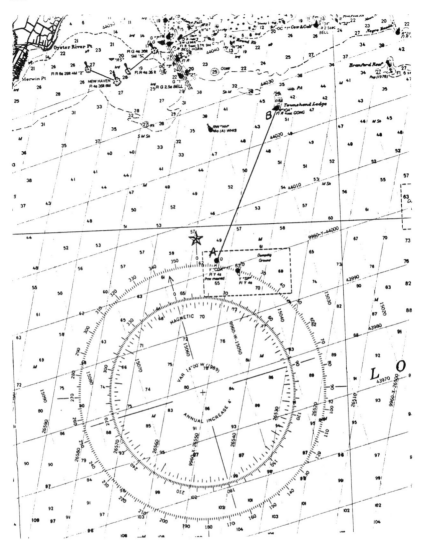

FIGURE 65
MEASURING DISTANCE

READING A CHART

Look at the section of a chart in figure 66. Buoys are shown as small diamonds with a dot or circle underneath to indicate their exact location. A purple color around the circle means it's a lighted buoy. The color of the diamond, usually red (actually pur-

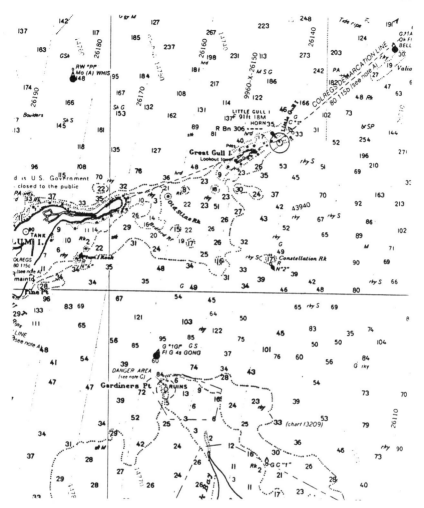

FIGURE 66

READING A CHART

ple on the chart), green, black and white, or all white, corresponds to the color of the buoy. Next to the diamond is a number in quotes, such as "23". Anything in quotes is written on the buoy. Even numbers are on red buoys and odd numbers are on green buoys. The chart will further describe the buoy as a bell, a gong, or a whistle depending on the type of sound they emit.

The information on Little Gull Island light in figure 66 is given next to it: "R Bn 306 · - - - F91ft 18M HORN". We interpret the information to mean it has a fixed white light 91 feet above mean

high sea level and has an 18 mile visibility. It sounds a horn during foggy periods and also is a radio beacon that transmits a dit-
dah-dah-dah signal on a frequency of 306 megahertz.

Below Little Gull Island on the chart is a diamond called
"Constellation Rock". It has R N"2" written near it. This means
it's a red nun buoy with the number two written on it. In the U.S.
we leave red buoys to starboard as we enter a harbor or sail from
a larger body of water to a smaller one. The simple phrase to
remember this fact is "Red-Right-Returning". Leave red buoys on
your starboard as you enter a harbor.

If you are cruising on the Intracoastal Waterway, the phrase
"red dirt, green sea" will help you remember which side to pass
the markers. The red markers are on the mainland side of the
channel, the dirt side, and the green markers are to seaward of
the channel.

There are many other items of information on the chart. Note
the colors. White areas are deep, navigable water, light blue areas
are usually under 20 feet deep, and green areas are out of the
water at low tide. The depths of the water are usually marked in
feet at mean low water. Extremely low water could mean depths
of four or five feet less than shown on the chart, so take that into
account. Along the east coast of the U.S. the tides are simidiurnal:
two high tides and two low tides in a 24 hour period. The tide
height changes about 25% the first and last two hours of a tide,
and about 50% during the middle two hours. In other words, if
you're in an area with a six foot tide, during the first two hours
the depth will drop 1.5 feet, the next two it will drop three feet
and last two, 1.5 feet. This is a factor to take into consideration if
it's necessary to cross a bar or a shoal that you know is too shallow for your boat at dead low tide, yet has deep enough water at
certain times during the tidal fall. The U.S. Government prints
the book "Tide Tables", giving the predicted times of high and
low water and the heights of the tide. On some charts the depths
(soundings) may be in meters or fathoms (six feet equals one
fathom), so check the explanation on the chart itself.

Also shown on charts are depth contours. These contour lines
connect all the areas of equal depth and are very useful in navigation with the depth finder.

On the beige part of the chart, indicating dry land, any object
which could be helpful in obtaining a navigational fix is located
and marked. Tanks, towers, conspicuous buildings, spires, and
others are all pinpointed. Always check your navigation. One of
the boats on our Tahiti cruise was steering for a church only to

find out it was the wrong church. Because they were keeping track they discovered their mistake before it became a problem.

VARIATION AND DEVIATION

Variation is described in Offshore Sailing School's Learn to Sail course. It is the angle between the geographic meridian (a line passing through both the geographic poles—north and south) and the local magnetic meridian; (a line passing through both magnetic poles). In other words, your compass will point to the magnetic north pole and at any given point this will be so many degrees to the west or east of true north which points to the geographic north pole. In a few spots on earth there is no variation and your magnetic compass will point to true north. Your chart will have the number of degrees of variation written on it for the given area.

Variation charts, such as figure 67, show how much variation there is at different locations. For instance, if your sailing between Cuba and the Florida Keys, the variation is five degrees west. Printed on most charts is a compass rose as in figure 68. It's a circle drawn on the chart graduated in 360 degrees. The outer circle gives you the true north direction. The inner circle on the compass rose is called the magnetic rose. The variation of the locality is easy to see by the angular difference of these two circles. The variation is also written at the center of the compass rose along with the annual rate of change. For example, "VAR 14° 00'W (1989) ANNUAL INCREASE 4' " reads "the variation is fourteen degrees, no minutes west as of the year 1989 with an annual increase of four minutes per year observed." You would have to apply the annual rate according to the date and age of the chart. This usually doesn't amount to much, but the careful navigator will at least be aware of this fact.

Deviation is the compass error caused by the metal on the boat that attracts the compass needle. On sailboats it rarely amounts to much, but it should be taken into account for accuracy even if it's only a degree. This error is measured when a compass adjuster "swings" your compass and, by the use of magnets, reduces the error caused by the magnetic pull of metal on the boat. It's the difference in direction the compass needle should point to, taking variation into account, and the direction it does point. The adjuster may not be able to correct all the deviation so will make a deviation table. This shows you the deviation for various

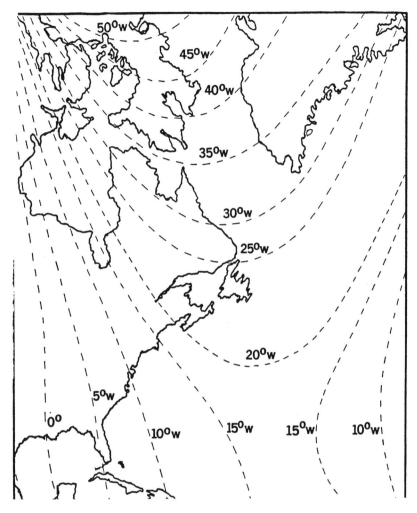

FIGURE 67

VARIATION CHARTS SHOW THE AMOUNT AT ANY LOCATION

boat headings. If deviation is small enough to be of little concern, say one or two degrees, assume your compass error will be equal to variation alone. Then you can take all your bearings and courses in magnetic readings and, being careful to use only the inner circle of the compass rose (the magnetic rose), plot directly.

You can determine your deviation in a less formal manner and correct it yourself. Place your boat next to a navigational aid with a known position such as a buoy. Draw a line on your chart north

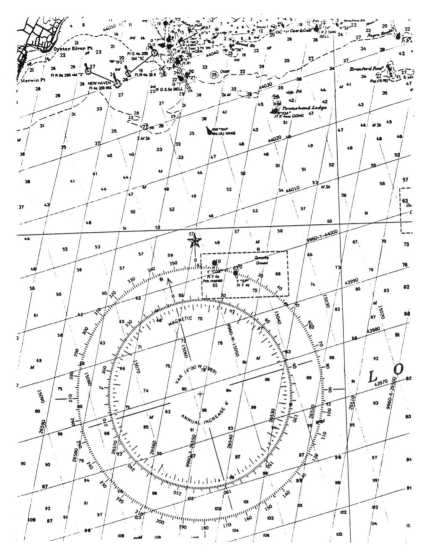

FIGURE 68

MAGNETIC AND TRUE READINGS ON A COMPASS ROSE

from the buoy (allowing for variation) and note which landmark in the distance the line passes through. Point your boat at the same landmark and see what your compass reads. The difference is deviation. By adjusting the magnets on the side of the compass, reduce the deviation by one-half. Then head east and determine the deviation in that direction. Reduce it by one-half by adjusting the magnets on the front and back of the compass. Continue with south, then west and then repeat the process all over again until most of the deviation is gone.

Both variation and deviation errors are expressed as either easterly errors (the compass needle points to the east of north) or westerly errors (the compass needle points to the west of north). They can be combined. For instance, if the variation is 10° E and the deviation is 2° W, the net compass error is 8° E. If the variation is 8° W and deviation is 1° W, the net error is 9° W.

By combining the errors we can use a very simple acronym to determine direction: CADET, which stands for Compass, Add East for True. In other words, if you have your compass heading, just add any easterly combined compass errors to obtain true heading. By just remembering CADET, all the rest falls into place logically. If you add easterly errors, you subtract westerly errors. If you have a true course from the chart and you want to know what compass course to steer, you reverse the procedure and subtract easterly errors and add westerly errors.

Let's say you have taken a bearing on a lighthouse to obtain your line of position. It bears 276°. Your deviation is 1° E and your variation is 7° E. Your chart does not have a magnetic compass rose on it, only a true one. You add 8° to 276° to get a true bearing of 284° which you plot on the chart.

Once you have determined your position, you set a new course for your boat, walk the parallel rulers over to the true compass rose and determine that your true course is 093°. What will be the course the helmsman will steer using your compass aboard? With a compass error of 8° E, we subtract it from 093° because we are going from true to compass, not compass to true as in the acronym, CADET. The answer is 085°.

DEAD RECKONING

Your "dead reckoning position" (DR) is the position determined by applying your course and distance from a previously determined position. There are a number of theories how it came to be called "dead" reckoning. One is that it's short for "deduced" reckoning because your position is being deducted from the input of your speed and distance. That "dead" was "ded" in middle English lends some credence to this theory. At the opposite end of the theory spectrum is that "dead" means "exact" as in a "dead shot" or "dead ahead". Dead reckoning, therefore, is as exact a reckoning of position as can be obtained with the variables existing.

A third and more intriguing possibility is that it comes from the log used on early sailing ships called a "chip log". It was made from a triangular chip of wood with lines from each corner that met a few feet away where they were attached to a single towline. The result was like a sea anchor that remained stationary when in the water. Along the towline were equally spaced knots and the line was coiled on a spindle much like that used to fly a kite. To measure the speed of the sailing ship, the chip log was put over the side and the line ran out. A 28 second sand glass was turned upside down and the number of knots that passed through the crewman's fingers by the time the sand ran out was equal to the number of nautical miles the ship was traveling per hour. So, though the knots originally were units of distance, they soon became known as units of speed with a built in sense of "per hour" which is why we never say "knots per hour". If five knots passed through his fingers, to say "five knots per hour" would be inaccurate because it was five knots in 28 seconds, the equivalent of five nautical miles in one hour. "Dead reckoning" most likely came from reckoning your position from the point where your chip log was dead in the water since you didn't measure your speed all the time—only when you wanted to update your position (or if there was a significant change in wind strength).

BEARINGS

Now you are ready to determine your position with a series of bearings transferred to your chart. In taking bearings in order to obtain a fix, the primary concern is to correctly identify a shore-based object or aid to navigation and locate this on the chart. A bearing taken on a building is fine, but unless this building is indicated on the chart it is useless to you. Study the chart looking for prominent objects in your vicinity. Best objects would be lighthouses, buoys, buildings or tangents of a prominent landmark or hill. Try to find these by looking carefully at the shoreline or known objects (recently passed navigational aids are a good place to start, such as channel buoys). Pick at least two objects that have a good angular separation. Two objects 90 degrees apart would be perfect, but rarely the case. In doing this, you have actually fixed the boat's position by "eyeball" navigation and you really just need to verify your position by more positive means.

Quickly sight across your steering compass or use a hand bearing compass to take your bearings. Observe the bearing closest to your bow or stern first as this will change the slowest. Then take the bearing closest to your beam and note the time to the nearest minute. Write these down and plot these lines on the chart. Using parallel rulers or triangles transfer the angles from the compass rose over to the object observed. Where these lines cross should be your position at the time of the fix, not at the present moment. You were there five minutes or so ago when you took the bearings. Make sure you write the time of the fix on the chart.

PLOTTING

Since sailboats are subject to the vagaries of the wind it's very difficult to set a particular course and speed in order to end up at a desired destination on a given schedule. Of course you can set an initial course and determine your ETA (estimated time of arrival) based on the speed you are making through the water adjusted for current, which gives you your speed and course over the bottom. But if the wind dies you won't make the speed you based your calculations on and you'll spend longer in the current which will require a course adjustment. If the wind shifts, your speed may change because you're on a different point of sailing, either faster or slower, even if the wind velocity doesn't change. The wind may shift further so you no longer lay the course you originally desired and have to beat for your destination. In short, you are constantly updating your position as you sail along and are forever changing the course to your destination. The navigator who doesn't keep careful track of his DR plot will get lost.

First we must start from a known position. We plot our course to the destination and after we have traveled awhile we plot the distance we have covered on the course we've been steering and mark it as our dead reckoning position with the time. We use the 24-hour clock in navigation, so 1515 in figure 69 is 3:15 p.m. Just add 12 hours to any p.m. time to get the 24-hour clock time. Always use four digits so 9:18 a.m. is marked 0918. Courses are written with three digits as 093 in the diagram. If it was written "93" a person reading another's writing might mistake a line or a smudge and read "193" or "293". We add "M" to the course to show it's magnetic or "T" for true. If you're using a chart with a magnetic compass rose and courses drawn on it are always magnetic, you may start deleting the "M".

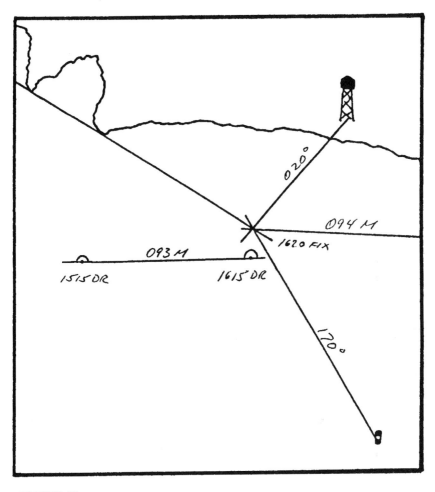

FIGURE 69

NOTE THE LOP TAKEN WHEN TWO POINTS COME IN LINE

We usually know two of three variables when we try to determine our position. Since we started at a known location and kept track of our speed and time run in a particular direction, we can figure out the distance. We measure the distance from the first location in the direction we have been sailing and determine the second location. These are simple Speed-Time-Distance problems. I have found them to be difficult for many people to remember, so there's a method that may be of help. Imagine a road sign in a town that says "D Street". But the sign is contracted to look like this: $\frac{D}{ST}$. Now put your thumb over the variable you want to find and what remains is the formula to find it. For instance, if you want speed, put your thumb over the "S" and what remains ($\frac{D}{T}$) tells you the formula is distance divided by time. To find "D" (distance) the formula is ST or speed times time. To find "T" (time) the formula is $\frac{D}{S}$ or distance divided by speed. Just remember "D Street".

In noting the time of your fixes or taking bearings, use minutes evenly divided by six. For example, use 06, 12, 18, 24, 30 etc. for your time, because 06 minutes equals 0.1 hours, 12 minutes equals 0.2 hours, 18 minutes equals 0.3 hours and so on. This makes your time even tenths of an hour and your speed, time and distance formula becomes easier to work.

To continue the plot, an hour after your first DR you update your position and discover three good landmarks or navigational aids to make bearings from. In figure 69 a radio tower marked on the chart bears 020°, a buoy bears 170° and a point of land has just obscured another point of land behind it. I use the third method all the time because you don't have to take a bearing and be subject to the possible errors caused by the compass swinging or by your parallel rulers slipping, etc. Just watch for two islands or points of land to come into line. Note the time. Then on your chart, locate these objects and align them with a straight edge, draw a line and there is your bearing; no compass required. It's a simple procedure, but very accurate and fast. Each of these bearings is a line of position to the object. Where two or more LOP's cross you have a "fix". You plot the bearings on the chart and get a small triangle. If you're lucky you may get all three lines to cross exactly the same spot. Nevertheless, a small triangle is accurate enough a position to call it a fix. Just mark a dot representing your position in the middle of the triangle, note the time and plot a new course to your destination, in this case 094M. If you have a log that reads the number of miles you have been sailing, it's always good to note the log reading on the chart at the time of the fix. Also, if you have a fathometer, check the depth of the water at the time of the fix and compare it to the depth shown on the chart for that location. This can confirm the accuracy of the fix. Use the fathometer for all DR plots also.

As you continue along the coast, there's a point of land ahead with some rocks off of it. You want to be sure to be far enough off the point to avoid them. There are various ways of accomplishing this. One is to use a sextant on the object and consult tables that tell you your distance off. Another is to use a range finder. However, you must know the height of the object which isn't a problem with a navigational light since their height is usually written on the chart or is at least listed in the government printed light list. Then describe an arc with a compass (as in figure 70) that encompass all the rocks and hazards. Let's say it's half a mile in this case. Mark it down as a danger range of 0.5 NM (nautical miles) and make sure that your range finder readings keep you outside this distance off the object. There's an excellent device called the "KVH DataScope" that will record up to ten very accurate bearings and will also give your range from objects of known height.

If you do not have a method such as the DataScope to measure your distance off, there are ways to stay clear of the rocks. Keep careful track of your course and speed. Plot a bearing on a landmark such as the lighthouse in figure 70. If you know you're sailing six knots and it's been five minutes between two bearings, you will have sailed half a mile. After five minutes of sailing, take and plot a second bearing. Place your dividers so the points are half a mile apart. Set your parallel rulers on the compass course of your boat's heading and run them across the two bearings until the dividers show the bearings to be half a mile apart. Then draw your course line and see if you clear the rocks. Remember that an adverse current means you won't have sailed half a mile in five minutes and you could very well be closer to shore than you estimated. In a fair current the opposite is true.

Figure 70 shows a method sometimes used to determine distance off an object. A bearing is taken relative to the bow of the

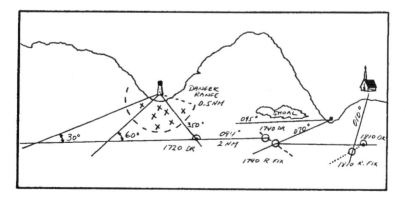

FIGURE 70

DANGER RANGE

boat (called a "relative bearing"). Let's say it's 30 degrees. When that bearing becomes double, 60 degrees, the distance you have sailed between the two sightings equals the distance to the object from your boat when you took the second bearing. It's called "doubling the angle". Another is called "bow and beam" bearings. Take a bearing when the object is 45 degrees off the bow of the boat. When the object is abeam, 90 degrees from the boat, the distance run from the time of taking the first bearing equals the distance to the object when abeam.

Continue on the trip along the shore in figure 70, you have taken a DR position at 1720 after sailing an hour from the previous fix. You have combined it with a bearing on the lighthouse of 350M, but it's not a fix because it's only one LOP, not two or more. You know there's a shoal that you must stay seaward of so you draw a line on the chart from the light on the next point that just clears the shoal. This line turns out to be 095° and is called the "danger bearing". Any bearing we subsequently take of the light that is 094° or lower keeps you clear of the shoal. If you take a bearing and it's 096° or higher, you are inshore of the 095° danger bearing and could possibly hit the shoal.

You are still sailing six knots and twenty minutes later at 1740 you take a bearing on the light and find it bears 070°. You know you have sailed a course of 094° and have sailed two nautical miles in twenty minutes. Your DR doesn't cross with the new bearing. Advance your first bearing two miles so it runs through the 1740 DR and is parallel (350 degrees) to the first bearing (the dotted line). The point where it intersects your bearing on the second object is called a "running fix". Mark it "1740 R Fix" and continue your 094° heading from that new fix. Half an hour (three nautical miles) later at 1810 you take a bearing on a church ashore and find it to be 010°. Your 1810 DR doesn't coincide with the bearing. Advance your second bearing (070°) three miles to the 1810 DR (the dotted lines) and the point it crosses the bearing on the church is your 1810 running fix.

OTHER FIXES

Keep in mind some of the various types of fixes available to you:

1. Bearing and fathometer. Sailing along some coasts the depth contours are fairly steep and roughly parallel to the coast. By combining a radio direction finder bearing or visual bearing

that's relatively perpendicular to the shore with a depth sounding that's roughly parallel to the shore, we get an approximate fix.

2. Bearing and distance. Take a bearing on a landmark on the chart and measure the distance from it by a DataScope or other device. The bearing is a line of position and the distance crosses it giving a fix.

3. A visual bearing and distance off determined by contour heights. All charts show the topography of the land masses. The height and steepness of the hills is shown by numbers and topographical contours.

Until I started to look closely at these contours on the chart, many sections of the shoreline looked like many others. When the contour lines are close together, indicating a steep slope, it's quite often easy to spot the hill it represents. The heights of the peaks are usually marked on the chart. Of two nearby summits, one may be 400 feet high and the other, 600 feet high. When you look at the shore, the perspective of the two summits to one another can give you a good idea of your geographical relationship to them. Use the known height of the peak with a distance measuring device to get the distance off. Then cross the bearing line of position at that distance to get a fix.

HELPFUL NAVIGATION TIPS

Since the lubber line of the compass is in line with your boat's bow, a simple and accurate bearing can be taken by just pointing the boat at the landmark or buoy whose bearing is desired. This works well even if you have to alter your course slightly to place the object dead ahead.

Another secret to safe navigation is to be very skeptical of your work. Once a fix is plotted, check by looking around to see if it makes sense. According to your position, do nearby objects appear in the proper perspective? Is that island really on your starboard bow as your fix shows? This is the type of reasoning you follow to check yourself. If the fix indicates a large change of course that seems strange (as if you had been in a current or making excessive leeway), take the bearings over again and replot the fix to confirm your position.

Nothing beats reading the number right off a buoy if it's close enough in order to verify that it's the right one. Once you've navigated awhile in fog, low visibility, and current, buoys that seem to confirm your position often turn out to be wrong ones on closer inspection. If you don't check the number and otherwise confirm your position, you might make a course alteration on the assumption that your navigation is correct and really end up in trouble. Remember that buoys for two harbors may look alike and be numbered the same. You could be entering the wrong harbor if you're way off. If you aren't sure, quickly plot a second fix to check the first, and so on. With practice you will gain confidence in your work and will more easily be able to catch mistakes before they can place you in danger.

Many find reading the small print on charts increasingly difficult with advancing age. One great little trick is to turn a pair of binoculars upside-down, put the eye end *very* close to the print and look through the wrong end (one side only). The print will be magnified many times.

Another trick is helpful if you're sailing south through a channel marked with a number of buoys. Turn the chart upside-down so the chart course is aimed the same direction as your bow. It's easier to keep track of the buoys you're passing.

If you've taken a large-scale chart on deck because you're following a channel close to land, be sure to have enough of it unfolded to navigate properly. I've watched people steering for a point of land thinking they had it pinpointed on the chart, when actually they were steering for land that was under the next fold of the chart.

There rarely is harm in throttling back on the engine and making a circle if you're powering into a strange harbor and are unsure of your location or that of the moorings or docks. It's far better to stop and get your bearings than to charge ahead blindly.

CURRENT

Current comes with tidal depth changes, and is quite a large factor in navigation as the current velocity becomes a large percentage of the boat's speed. Therefore, it's particularly a factor in sailing. A sailboat averaging 5 knots may be sailing in a current 20% to 40% (1 to 2 knots) of its speed. The speed of the current is called its "drift" and the direction to which it flows is its "set". For instance, sailing in a two knot westerly current, you have a two knot drift and westerly set.

The Tidal Current Tables printed by the U.S. Government give the maximum flood and ebb current and the time when the current changes direction. Tidal Current Charts are printed for twelve bodies of water on the east and west coasts, and are very handy in navigation and planning a cruise. These two are combined in a publication called the Eldridge Tide and Pilot Book, which covers the northeast coast, and Reed's Almanac.

Let's say we locate our present position on the chart and find that the current is 0.5 knots in a direction of about 270 degrees True. We transfer this information to a chart as in figure 71. We are at point A sailing on a course of 360 degrees T. First we draw

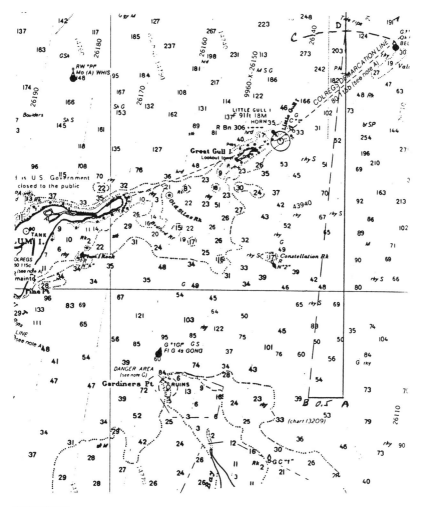

FIGURE 71

WORKING OUT CURRENT PROBLEMS

line AB one-half mile long, indicating the effect of the current on the boat in one hour. Next we take the boat speed (5 knots in this case) and describe arc C to intersect the course line at point D. Line BD will be the course to steer, and A to D will be our progress over the bottom toward our destination in one hour and our speed made good in knots. If the current velocity or direction changes over the period of time it takes us to reach our destination, we can use an average current for our calculations.

Rather than transfer these courses all over to our position on the chart, the same course to steer can be determined by drawing the current diagram right on the compass rose on the chart in the same manner.

When your DR includes allowances for current and leeway most navigators call it an "estimated position" and mark it "EP" on the chart with the time. Some navigators even draw two separate plots, one DR and one EP until a fix can be obtained.

GPS

GPS or 'Global Positioning System' makes use of satellites to determine your position. It's a remarkable advancement, but, as with everything in sailing, needs to be worked carefully. It tends to make navigators very lazy, because of the confidence they have in the machine. If the boat's battery power is lost or the GPS malfunctions, you are without its services. If you have failed to practice the old fashioned way of navigating, not only are you lost, but you have reduced ability to navigate the normal way from lack of practice. It is always a good idea to update your position on a paper chart continually, so you can continue on after a GPS failure.

Another problem arises when the navigator gets a bearing (course) for the destination from the GPS and doesn't plot it carefully on the chart to make sure the course doesn't pass over shoal areas, through buoys or even over land. Most navigators are careful enough to check the course initially, but fail to are-plot it a few hours later when, due to leeway, current, wind direction changes or whatever, the GPS shows a different course to the destination. The tendency is to forget the original course and constantly change the course to that which the GPS tells you is the direction to your destination. Because of such sloppiness you may end up on the rocks. If your GPS has a chart plotter, such mistakes are rare, however.

THE LOG

The "ship's logbook" is the key source of plotting information for the navigator. Rather than plotting all the time, the crew records the course and speed of the boat, so the navigator can update the information every few hours. Close to land and on short trips and out at sea, every hour is sufficient. You might ask how you can give a navigator a course and speed for a half hour period when you have been swinging twenty degrees in following seas and surging from five to ten knots. The answer is to give your best judgement of the average for the period. You'll be amazed at how accurate the results are when you finally get a fix even after ten or twelve hours of averaging. A modern electronic log records the nautical miles covered. Record the miles run in the logbook every half hour or hour. This backs up your estimate of speed.

When the navigator decides to update the boat's position, he or she can either plot each log entry or average them together. Averaging will give a fairly accurate course, but not distance. The plot is recorded on the chart with time.

NAVIGATION IN EUROPE

One of the most important things to remember when cruising anywhere other than the United States and the Caribbean is that "Red, Right, Returning" doesn't work. Red buoys are on your port side when entering harbors and green to starboard. This makes more sense than our system, because it coincides with the navigation lights on the boat, red being on the port side. The starboard hand marks are more conical shaped than the port hand marks, just as the cans and nuns in the states.

Another system of marks, called "cardinal" marks is also common in Europe. These marks show the direction (north, south, east or west) from the mark that the best navigable water lies. They are shown in figure 72. The north mark has both arrows pointing up or north, the south arrows point downward or south, one east arrow points north and one points south and the west mark is the opposite (they point at each other). If you don't use these often enough to memorize them, keep the diagram handy when sailing overseas.

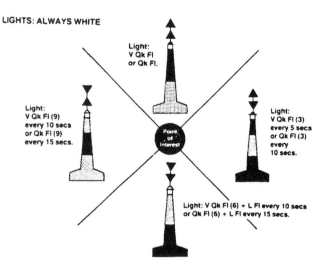

LIGHTS: ALWAYS WHITE

Light:
V Qk Fl
or Qk Fl.

Light:
V Qk Fl (9)
every 10 secs
or Qk Fl (9)
every 15 secs.

Point
of
Interest

Light:
V Qk Fl (3)
every 5 secs
or Qk Fl (3)
every
10 secs.

Light: V Qk Fl (6) + L Fl every 10 secs
or Qk Fl (6) + L Fl every 15 secs.

FIGURE 72

TYPICAL MARKS FOUND IN EUROPE

COURTESY

Yachting has been steeped with a long tradition of courtesy. Sailing off the coast of England, when you pass another boat a crew member will run aft and dip the yacht ensign (or sometimes the national flag) to half-staff. In response you must dip yours.

Though the above is a little more than we're apt to find sailing along our coast, we, too, have our courtesies to adhere to. For instance, you always ask permission of the owner or skipper before setting foot on his boat. You wear rubber-soled shoes or sneakers or you take your leather shoes off before you step aboard. The latter can scratch the deck. Some skippers will allow them, but ask first.

When sailing, you should stay well clear of any boats that are racing, even if you have the right of way. The same holds true of powerboats that are trolling for fish.

It is proper to "make colors" (raise and lower the flags) at 0800 and sunset respectively. The yacht ensign or national flag is raised first followed by the yacht club burgee and owner's private signal. Flags are lowered in inverse order.

One of the most important things to remember is the little courtesies extended to other people aboard. There is nothing more infuriating than a person who won't do their share of the "dirty work"—washing salt spray off the decks, washing the dishes, cooking, changing sails, and the many other things involved in cruising. Anyone who expects to be waited on had better go out and hire a servant. Whenever you use the head, leave it clean for the next person.

Mentioned before, but worth reiterating, is the courtesy of tying off your halyards at night to keep them from slapping the mast. They can make an awful racket that disturbs the peace of a quiet anchorage. Also, if you anchor later than another boat and find yourself swinging too close, you should be the one to move. If you were there first, they should move.

A good rule whenever you charter or borrow a sailboat is to leave it in as good (or better) condition than you received it. People don't seem to have pride in keeping sailboats shipshape anymore, nor do they derive pride from proper seamanship. We hope that we can instill such pride in the students that sail with us.

APPENDIX A

A	ALFA	J	JULIET	S	SIERRA
B	BRAVO	K	KILO	T	TANGO
C	CHARLIE	L	LIMA	U	UNIFORM
D	DELTA	M	MIKE	V	VICTOR
E	ECHO	N	NOVEMBER	W	WHISKEY
F	FOXTROT	O	OSCAR	X	X-RAY
G	GOLF	P	PAPA	Y	YANKEE
H	HOTEL	Q	QUEBEC	Z	ZULU
I	INDIA	R	ROMEO		

The Complete Colgate
Sailing Library

Steve Colgate on Sailing by Steve Colgate. 416 pages of incomparable information. From basic terminology to cruising tips and racing, the most comprehensive book available. $29.95.

Colgate's Basic Sailing by Steve Colgate. Critics call it the best. Steve's style makes it easy. $9.95.

Advanced Sailing by Steve Colgate. Seamanship, advanced sail trim, theory and navigation. $9.95.

Steve Colgate on Cruising by Steve Colgate. The complete guide to bareboat chartering. $13.95.

Fast Track to Cruising by Steve and Doris Colgate based on the Offshore Sailing School course by the same name. It's a complete guide on how to go from novice to cruise-ready in seven days. $22.95.

VIDEO TAPES
Learn to Sail Video Tape. 106 minutes of step by step basic-to-intermediate instruction with Steve Colgate and film stars Sam Jones and Audrey Landers. $29.95. VHS

ORDER TOLL FREE 800-221-4326

Or mail to: Offshore Sailing School
16731 McGregor Blvd.
Ft. Myers, FL 33908

NAME: (please print) _____

ADDRESS: _____

CITY: _____ STATE: _____ ZIP _____

HOME PHONE: _____ DAYTIME PHONE: _____

TITLE	PRICE
Shipping	
6% Sales Tax (Florida Residents Only)	
TOTAL	

Method of Payment: [ ] Check [ ] Visa [ ] Mastercard [ ] Amex

Account Number: _____ Exp. Date _____

Signature: _____